Norman Rockwell's
Four Freedoms

Images that inspire a nation

Norman Rockwell's
Four Freedoms

Images that inspire a nation

Stuart Murray and James McCabe

with essays on the Four Freedoms by

John Frohnmayer
Theodore H. Evans
James MacGregor Burns
Brian Urquhart
William J. vanden Heuvel

Foreword by Laurie Norton Moffatt

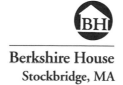

Berkshire House
Stockbridge, MA

The
Norman
Rockwell
Museum
at Stockbridge

Berkshire House Publishers
PO Box 297
Stockbridge, Massachusetts 01262

The Norman Rockwell Museum
Stockbridge, Massachusetts 01262

Copyright © 1993 by Berkshire House Publishers.
All rights reserved.

No part of this publication may be reproduced,
stored in a retrieval system, or transmitted, in any
form or by any means — electronic, mechanical,
photocopying, recording, or otherwise — without the
prior permission in writing of the publishers and the
copyright holder.

Library of Congress Cataloging-in-Publication Data
Murray, Stuart, 1948-
      Norman Rockwell's four freedoms : images that
inspire a nation / Stuart Murray and James McCabe ;
with essays by John Frohnmayer . . . [et al.].
          p.   cm.
      Includes bibliographical references.
      ISBN 0-936399-43-0 : $24.95.
      ISBN 0-936399-42-2 (pbk.) : $14.95
      1. Rockwell, Norman, 1894-1978—Criticism and
interpretation. 2. Civil rights in art. I. McCabe, James,
1955-   . II. Title.
ND237.R68M87 1993
759.13—dc20   93-3545
                                                    CIP

Printed in Mexico.

10 9 8 7 6 5 4 3 2 1

For my children,
who also love the work
of Norman Rockwell.

S.M.

To Susan,
who has all the good ideas.

J.M.

As the Second World War raged in 1942, Norman Rockwell painted four images that were to become enduring national symbols. His inspiration was President Franklin Delano Roosevelt's 1941 address to Congress which set out the four fundamental freedoms enunciated by the Allied powers on behalf of people everywhere. Eventually, in the minds of many, Rockwell's images became interchangeable with Roosevelt's concepts. The president's ideals were permanently captured in these pictures which are today the cornerstone of the collections of the Norman Rockwell Museum at Stockbridge.

The fascinating story behind these paintings, the ideas that inspired them, and their powerful impact on our nation is told in these pages. But the story of the Four Freedoms did not end with the end of the war in 1945. The Freedoms remain no less compelling or relevant today. In recent decades millions of visitors to the Norman Rockwell Museum have responded to these paintings. Contemporary political cartoonists reemploy Rockwell's images to influence public opinion. Textbook publishers illustrate civics lessons with them. Even the Disney Company has produced a lighthearted parody placing its cartoon characters in Rockwell's Thanksgiving pose.

President Roosevelt and Norman Rockwell addressed, each in his own way, a profound question of citizenship: what are the national goals which justify asking citizens to make ultimate sacrifices? Both men rose above propaganda or appeals to a nationalism fueled by hatred and sought, instead, to define values which would unite citizens and could bind nations to each other.

When the paintings were first published in the *Saturday Evening Post* in 1943, each was accompanied by an essay by a distinguished writer discussing that freedom in the context of that time. Now, on the occasion of the 50th anniversary of Rockwell's paintings, five distinguished contemporary commentators have written about the relevance and meaning of these freedoms in today's society and today's world conditions. The essence of their message is that though much has changed and today's issues are not those of a world at war, the fundamental principles still apply, and have the power to inspire people today as they did 50 years ago.

Franklin Roosevelt and Norman Rockwell left the world an enduring legacy of principles that continue to inspire democracy and human compassion throughout the world.

Laurie Norton Moffatt
Director
The Norman Rockwell Museum
Stockbridge, Massachusetts

Preface and Acknowledgments

Thanks to Thomas Rockwell, whose response to the manuscript was invaluable for the integrity of this work; to managing editor Sarah Novak, whose professionalism and thoughtfulness made her a pleasure to work with; to the staff of the Norman Rockwell Museum at Stockbridge for their assistance with the research for this book while under the intense pressure of building the Rockwell museum and installing the new exhibits; to David Emblidge, who saw from the start the importance of telling the story of the Four Freedoms; to the staff of the Chatham Public Library in Chatham, New York, for their unfailing kindness and helpfulness; and finally, thanks to my co-author James McCabe. Jim's conscientious response to the manuscript was required at an extremely demanding time while he was conducting original research into the untold story of the Four Freedoms and the War Bond Show.

Stuart Murray
Chatham, New York

Most successful projects seem to have a center, a place where ideas and opportunities converge, and where there is a will to act on them. For this book, that center is the Norman Rockwell Museum at Stockbridge. As part of their program for a new museum building, I was curator for a new exhibition on Norman Rockwell's *Four Freedoms* and their role in the history of the home-front during World War Two. At the same time, Stuart Murray saw a great personal story in Rockwell's odyssey with the *Four Freedoms*. Working through the museum's neighbor, Berkshire House Publishers, this book moved from idea to undertaking in the office of Laurie Norton Moffatt, director of the museum, with the support of the Rockwell family.

The assistance of the museum has been essential to the project. Assistant Director of Education and Programs Maud Ayson and Curator Maureen Hart Hennessey and their staffs took on this effort while in the midst of the monumental process of building a new facility and moving the museum to it. Maud Ayson kept things on track, and kept me full of fresh ideas and approaches. Maureen Hart Hennessey was key to the success of the project: finding resources in her budget to support it, providing information and access to the outstanding collection of materials that make up the museum's archives, identifying important contacts and resources, and reading and fact-checking the manuscript. Her support, good will, and humor were unwavering.

It is no small effort making two visions of a book into one. Our editor at Berkshire House, Sarah Novak, kept the book moving forward, made sure we were working on the same story, and helped create a union of these two visions. Throughout the process she has been a pleasure to work with, keeping goals in focus, spirits up, and molehills from becoming mountains.

The Norman Rockwell Museum is the most important single resource for researching Norman Rockwell, having his personal papers as well much of his illustration legacy in its large collections. However, the 1943 fire in Rockwell's studio shortly after he completed the *Four Freedoms* destroyed many of the records he generated in creating those paintings. What remains was very important to the book. Rockwell's autobiographical account of his experiences with the Four Freedoms written with his son Thomas Rockwell continues to be the core of this story. Much of the rest of it comes from people and institutions around the country whose collections and remembrances have added to the story. The collections of the Franklin D. Roosevelt Library and Museum in Hyde Park, New

York, provided considerable insight into the relationship between Rockwell and the White House. A special thanks goes to Alycia Vivona for her help with the fine collection of posters. The National Archives' records from the Treasury and from the Office of War Information were critically important sources of both information and images. Archivist Bill Creech helped immensely with the Treasury records, which had only been recently organized, and with other materials. The Library of Congress had two important manuscript collections relating to the Office of War Information, the papers of Archibald MacLeish and Elmer Davis. Sawyer Library at Williams College was also helpful, and Lee Dalzell assisted in securing some of the images used in the book.

Most accounts of Rockwell seem to be filled with stories about people whose lives he touched, and this one is no exception. Many individuals contributed their recollections to this book. As always, Rockwell's Arlington neighbors were a great help, including Shirley Hoisington McTernan, Dorothy and Edgar Lawrence, and Gene Pelham. In addition, Susan Meyer's collection of interviews for her fine book *Rockwell's People* were a great help. Others had memories of Rockwell while he was at work on the *Four Freedoms*, including John Cullen Murphy and Joe Busciglio, and others contributed memories of the Four Freedoms War Bond Show, notably Fred Markland.

A number of non-traditional repositories also held resources used by this book. They include the Curtis Archives and The Saturday Evening Post Society, which have large holdings related to the *Saturday Evening Post*, and the Arlington Town Clerk Joyce Wyman, who unearthed a number of items relating to life in Arlington during the war. Strawbridge and Clothier, the retailer that hosted the Four Freedoms War Bond Show in Philadelphia, helped by locating information about that event. Douglas Bailey at the City of Burbank Records Center was very helpful in locating information on another Four Freedoms artist, Hugo Ballin.

John Frohnmayer, The Reverend Tad Evans, James MacGregor Burns, Brian Urquhart, and William vanden Heuvel have provided valuable perspective on the enduring power of these ideas and images. Finally, I would like to thank my co-author Stuart Murray for finding the story in this history.

James McCabe
Dearborn, Michigan

Part One

Franklin D. Roosevelt's Four Freedoms

President Franklin D. Roosevelt's "Four Freedoms," stated in his annual address to Congress on January 6, 1941, declared an increased commitment by the United States to the preservation of free societies around the world.

On New Year's Day, 1941, President Franklin Delano Roosevelt worked late into the night in his small, private study on the second floor of the White House. Roosevelt and three aides sat around a desk, each man with a draft copy of the president's annual address, which was to be delivered to Congress in a few days. The United States was once again in danger of being drawn into world war, and Roosevelt's address began by declaring that "at no previous time has American security been as seriously threatened from without as it is today."

A stenographer was on hand to take dictation and, along with Roosevelt's aides, she sat quietly as the president leaned back in a swivel chair and gazed thoughtfully at the ceiling. He was considering the choice of words for the closing of his speech. For a long time, Roosevelt said nothing, and as his staff waited for him to go on, the room became completely silent.

Roosevelt always worked personally on each draft of an important speech until satisfied with every word. He favored direct language that was both eloquent and easy to understand. During his first two terms as president, Roosevelt had explained his plans

President Roosevelt's edits to the Four Freedoms speech show his intent that the four freedoms become ideals "everywhere in the world."

FIFTH DRAFT

— 18 — 176

The first is freedom of speech and expression everywhere in the world.

The second is freedom of every person to worship God in his own way everywhere in the world.

The third is freedom from want — which translated into ~~international~~ *world* terms means economic understandings which will secure to every nation ~~everywhere~~ a healthy peace time life for its inhabitants — *everywhere in the world*

The fourth is freedom from fear — which translated into ~~international~~ *world* terms means a world-wide reduction of armaments to such a point and in such a thorough fashion that no nation ~~anywhere~~ will be in a position to commit an act of physical aggression against any neighbor — *anywhere in the world.*

That kind of a world is the very antithesis of the so-called "new order" which the dictators seek to create ~~at the point of a gun~~ *with the crash of a bomb* in Europe and in Asia.

To that "new order" we oppose the greater conception, the moral order. A good society is able to face schemes of world domination and foreign revolutions alike without fear. It has no need either for the one or for the other.

in periodic radio broadcasts known as "fireside chats." In his latest broadcast, just three days ago, he had declared that the United States must become the "arsenal of democracy" to supply Britain in her fight against the Axis powers of Germany and Italy.

In this "fireside chat" Roosevelt had warned that the Axis would attack America next if Britain, now under siege, were defeated. Britain's war needs, he had said, were an integral part of America's own defense. In European countries occupied by the Nazis, subjugated peoples had been given hope by this dramatic broadcast. Americans, too, were inspired, and telegrams to the White House had run a hundred to one in favor of the "arsenal of democracy" policy. Now, in his annual address, Roosevelt was about to ask Congress to carry out that policy.

Soon to be inaugurated for an unprecedented third term — after a decisive victory in November over the Republican candidate, Wendell L. Willkie — Roosevelt was at the height of political power. Re-election had confirmed the nation's support for his policy of doing everything short of actual combat to help the Allies. To many Americans, war with Germany and Italy — and perhaps with imperialistic Japan — seemed only a matter of time.

By now, this coming annual address to Congress was already well polished, almost ready to deliver; it said, "Enduring peace cannot be bought at the expense of other people's freedom." It called for lending or leasing war matériel to embattled Britain and her allies, to be repaid in kind after the war was over. With this speech, Roosevelt intended not only to present his "Lend-Lease" plan to Congress, but also to offer his vision of a better future world, in a time of peace. It was this vision of the future Roosevelt now pondered in silence.

As the others in the president's study waited for Roosevelt to speak, the silence grew almost heavy. "It was a long pause," remembered one of his aides, "so long that it began to become uncomfortable."

Then Roosevelt abruptly leaned forward in his chair and began dictating to the stenographer. He spoke slowly and decisively, and to the surprise of his aides, "the words seemed now to roll off his tongue as though he had rehearsed them many times to himself."

When, on January 6, the speech was given to the joint session of the Seventy-seventh Congress, scarcely a word of that original closing had been changed:

"In the future days, which we seek to make secure, we look forward to a world founded upon four essential human freedoms.

"The first is freedom of speech and expression — everywhere in the world.

"The second is freedom of every person to worship God in his own way — everywhere in the world.

"The third is freedom from want — which, translated into world terms, means economic understandings which will secure to every nation a healthy peacetime life for its inhabitants — everywhere in the world.

"The fourth is freedom from fear — which, translated into world terms, means a worldwide reduction of armaments to such a point and in such a thorough fashion that no nation will be in a position to commit an act of physical aggression against any neighbor — anywhere in the world.

"That is no vision of a distant millennium. It is a definite basis for a kind of world attainable in our own time and generation. That kind of world is the very antithesis of the so-called new order of tyranny which the dictators seek to create with the crash of a bomb.

"To that new order we oppose the great conception — the moral order."

Eleven months later, on December 7, 1941, the Japanese launched a surprise attack on the American naval base at Pearl Harbor, Hawaii, and within days the United States was at war with Japan and Germany and the other Axis countries.

By the summer of 1942, all of the nation's resources were directed toward mobilization for total war, but the daily headlines and bulletins made it clear that the conflict was going badly for the Allies. That month, Americans were grateful to hear of the main Japanese battle fleet being repulsed at Midway Island, but as yet no one knew this victory would mark the limit of Japanese expansion in the Pacific. They did know, however, that the carrier *Yorktown* had been lost in the fight. On the other side of the globe, most of

Europe was still a fortress-prison under the boot of Nazi Germany. Great Britain, besieged for two years, was holding out, but Russia appeared about to collapse, her cities lying in ruins.

America watched the Nazis arrest those who spoke out, restrict religious freedom, and bring terror and starvation to whole nations — and realized what defeat in this war could mean. Meanwhile, from day to day, ordinary Americans carried the heavy burden of mobilization. Millions of young people were away in military service, many already lost or missing in action. Thousands more were enlisting daily. Everywhere, factories roared at full blast, turning out war machines for America and its allies. Families saved scrap metal and rubber, bought government bonds, and planted victory gardens, while the radio played popular new songs that were full of confidence, yet looked forward to the troops coming home.

By now, President Roosevelt's four essential freedoms — Freedom of Speech, Freedom of Worship, Freedom from Want, and Freedom from Fear — were being widely publicized by the government as a way of explaining why America was fighting the war. Though the concepts behind them were still abstract and somewhat vague in people's minds, the president's four freedoms were well known across the country, even in small towns like Arlington, nestled in the mountains of Vermont.

That July in 1942 at least one Arlington resident was thinking deeply about the meaning of the four freedoms: the artist Norman Rockwell wanted to illustrate them, to show just what they meant to America. Rockwell was already one of the most famous illustrators in the United States and fully mature as an artist, but hard as he had tried to come up with the right images for Roosevelt's four freedoms, he had not been able to do it.

Any professional artist who kept up with current affairs in the art world knew the government was eager for artists' participation in the campaign to mobilize the nation for the war effort. Central to that campaign in the early months of the war was the message of the aims of the war — the "why we fight" message. Roosevelt's four freedoms emerged in the public mind as the ideological basis for the nation's involvement in the war, especially as opposed to Nazism, Fascism, and imperialism. Illustrations of these war effort themes would be reproduced by the hundreds of thousands as war posters — visualizations of a world worth fighting for. Labeled by some as outright war propaganda and by others as vital rallying points for the nation, images of these messages — including the four freedoms ideals — were meant to bring unity to the national war effort.

The concept of essential human freedoms had been included in the momentous Atlantic Charter in August, 1941, when in a shipboard conference President Roosevelt for the United States and Prime Minister Winston Churchill for Great Britain had declared their united vision for the future after the "final destruction of the Nazi tyranny."

Several times Rockwell had tried to read the Atlantic Charter, as he wrote in his autobiography, "thinking that maybe it contained the idea I was looking for. But I hadn't been able to get beyond the first paragraph."

The language of the Atlantic Charter had been so noble, he said, but he was "not noble enough" to illustrate it. "Besides, nobody I know is reading the proclamation either, despite all the fanfare and hullabaloo about it in the press and on the radio."

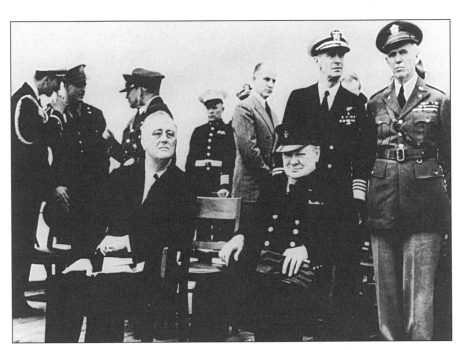

Roosevelt and Churchill's secret shipboard conference in the Atlantic Ocean off Newfoundland, Canada, resulted in the Atlantic Charter.

THE ATLANTIC CHARTER

*On August 14, 1941, P*RESIDENT *R*OOSEVELT *and* P*RIME* M*INISTER* C*HURCHILL,
at the conclusion of their mid-ocean conference, made the following joint declaration of "certain common principles in the national policies of their respective countries on which they base their hopes for a better future for the world."*

FIRST, their countries seek no aggrandizement, territorial or other;

SECOND, they desire to see no territorial changes that do not accord with the freely expressed wishes of the peoples concerned;

THIRD, they respect the right of all peoples to choose the form of government under which they will live; and they wish to see sovereign rights and self-government restored to those who have been forcibly deprived of them;

FOURTH, they will endeavor, with due respect for their existing obligations, to further the enjoyment by all States, great or small, victor or vanquished, of access, on equal terms, to the trade and to the raw materials of the world which are needed for their economic prosperity;

FIFTH, they desire to bring about the fullest collaboration between all nations in the economic field with the object of securing, for all, improved labor standards, economic advancement and social security;

SIXTH, after the final destruction of the Nazi tyranny, they hope to see established a peace which will afford to all nations the means of dwelling in safety within their own boundaries, and which will afford assurance that all the men in all the lands may live out their lives in freedom from fear and want;

SEVENTH, such a peace should enable all men to traverse the high seas and oceans without hindrance;

EIGHTH, they believe that all of the nations of the world, for realistic as well as spiritual reasons, must come to the abandonment of the use of force. Since no future peace can be maintained if land, sea or air armaments continue to be employed by nations which threaten, or may threaten, aggression outside of their frontiers, they believe, pending the establishment of a wider and permanent system of general security, that the disarmament of such nations is essential. They will likewise aid and encourage all other practicable measures which will lighten for peace-loving peoples the crushing burden of armaments.

Franklin D. Roosevelt
Winston S. Churchill

The Atlantic Charter was a statement of common principles for a better future for the world. Rockwell found the ideas noble, but difficult to portray in ordinary terms.

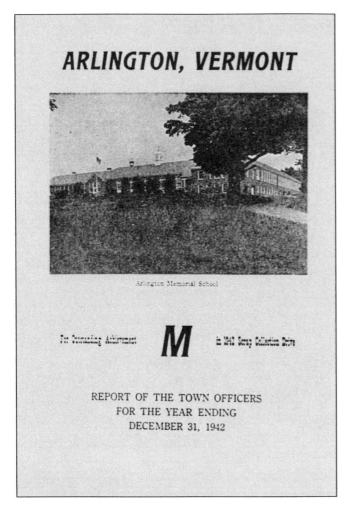

The cover of the Arlington town meeting report for 1942.

Rockwell "continued to stew over an idea. I tried this and that. Nothing worked. I juggled the Four Freedoms around in my mind, reading a sentence here, a sentence there, trying to find a picture. But it was so high-blown. Somehow I just couldn't get my mind around it."

Other well-known artists already had been commissioned by the government to paint murals of the four freedoms, to design stamps and prints, to create billboards, and to sculpt statues. Neoclassical, abstract, social realist, and expressionistic forms of the four freedoms were or soon would be in the works — most of them lofty images of eloquence and reverence, of bounty and militancy.

Such ideas did not work for Norman Rockwell.

In Arlington, overshadowed by war, life went on more or less as usual in mid-1942. At the annual town meeting most discussion was about local affairs, not the war. A new school was under construction and there was some spirited disagreement over how to go about it. As was usual with important community meetings in southern Vermont, many residents came to listen and to speak, and Rockwell occasionally could be found sitting in the audience.

Living in a colonial farmhouse near the village of Arlington, beside the winding Batten Kill river, Rockwell, too, went on with life as usual, despite the war. He and his wife Mary attended community meetings and covered-dish suppers, usually at the Grange; they swam in the river and visited with friends, ranging from farmers to doctors and including several other famous illustrators who lately had moved to the

Arlington area. Southern Vermont had an active community of artists centered in the Manchester-Dorset area, a dozen miles north of Arlington.

As always, Rockwell worked hard in the studio he had built in a converted barn behind the farmhouse. Yet, even though he accepted a tremendous workload, seldom turning down a commission, he took time to relax. Sometimes he went for long walks with his three young sons and Mary. On back roads, he would stop at a dairy barn to watch the milking, or linger by a fence to see a farmer pitch hay into a horse-drawn wagon.

In summertime, Rockwell sometimes strolled in the village of Arlington, a picturesque gathering of white clapboard and maples. These days, as he walked down Main Street — greeting occasional passersby and absently drawing on his ever-present pipe — he often thought about Franklin D. Roosevelt's four freedoms and how to paint them. He found them so broad and sweeping, however, that he wondered whether they could be captured in a picture.

In town, Rockwell might meet acquaintances who also had been his models, like stocky Jim Edgerton, a young dairy farmer, or Jim's son, Buddy, the handsome boy who in later years posed as a Boy Scout, but never joined up. There was Dr. George Russell, who obliged the illustrator by posing as a country doctor, and Arlington's sheriff, Harvey McKee, who had appeared as a country lawman. Also around town was a friendly fellow named Bob Buck, a sawmill hand who modeled as the easygoing draftee named Willie Gillis.

Many others in the vicinity of Arlington were (or would become) models for Rockwell: people named Crofut, Zimmer, Martin, Benedict, Hoyt, Squires, Harrington, Robertson, and Hall. Carl Hess, who owned the gas station in West Arlington, had a clear-eyed look that interested the artist, but Hess had not yet modeled for him.

Norman Rockwell was happy in Arlington. A native of Manhattan, he had moved here permanently in 1940 from suburban New Rochelle, a wealthy town that seemed full of professional artists working for New York and Philadelphia publishers. Though he had always loved the country, Rockwell had spent most of his life in New York City or its crowded suburbs. He was a man who worked eight hours a day, often seven days a week, so the years living near the city had been constantly busy. Then, in 1938, it was time for a change.

After twenty years in New Rochelle, "I was restless," he wrote in his autobiography. "The town seemed tinged with everything that had happened to me" in that time, including a divorce and several unsettling years of stepping out with a fast, social-climbing crowd.

As he looked around himself in New Rochelle, he mused: "The studio was somehow musty; the events . . . were piled up in the corners — all the paintings I'd done, the parties, things I liked to remember, and some I didn't — gathering dust. I had the feeling that part of my life had ended."

In mid-1938, on their first visit to Arlington and only just beginning to think about moving there, Norman and Mary Rockwell stayed the night at the Colonial Inn.

"After supper we sat on the wide lawn before the inn, watching the dusk gather beneath the huge elms which lined the street and around the gray stone church and the old graveyard across the way. After a while the stars came out in the luminous blue sky above the dark mountains."

The Rockwells soon bought a remote farm and sixty acres on the Batten Kill, a favorite of trout fishermen. In a year or two they felt like locals, having "endured the winter — snow, bad roads, 35 degrees below zero five mornings in a row — along with everybody else."

From the start, Rockwell was a good neighbor whom residents recall as being "one of us," even though Arlington was the typically close-knit New England town that customarily required twenty years before it fully accepted an outsider. Then again, Norman Rockwell was not really an outsider to any community in America. He, or at least his work, was part of the family.

During the past twenty-six years, Rockwell had painted more than two hundred covers for the weekly *Saturday Evening Post*, the top magazine in the country for illustrators, with the best writers and read by millions of loyal subscribers. Boy Scout calendars with Rockwell paintings hung in thousands of homes, appearing each year on the wall like the change of seasons, familiar and expected.

Since his first paying illustration jobs in 1912, Rockwell's combination of genius and meticulous skill had brought him to the pinnacle of his profession. His name was a household word, his pictures part of the fabric of American culture. It was said he had made more than a million dollars painting for the *Post, Boys' Life, Literary Digest, Ladies' Home Journal*, and *American* magazine, as well as for advertising agencies. He could tell a story with a picture better than anyone, depicting American characters in uniquely American settings.

In the summer of 1942, life and career were very good to Norman Rockwell, but he was not satisfied with his success. He was seeking something more, wanting to create a picture "bigger than a war poster, make some statement about why the country was fighting the war." Roosevelt's four freedoms had nagged at Rockwell all that spring and into summer, so that "at the time I couldn't concentrate properly," for they "occupied the better part of my brain."

How could he "take the Four Freedoms out of the noble language and put them in terms everybody can understand?" Ever since the United States entered the war in December, Rockwell and his close friend Mead Schaeffer (another top *Post* illustrator also living in Arlington and like Rockwell too old to enlist) had intended to do their part by painting posters for the government. They had worked up several ideas in rough format and were planning to set off for Washington soon.

"The only thing that was delaying us was me," Rockwell wrote in his autobiography. He was not satisfied with any of the poster ideas he had sketched out — none was of the four freedoms. As yet he had simply been unable to get started with them.

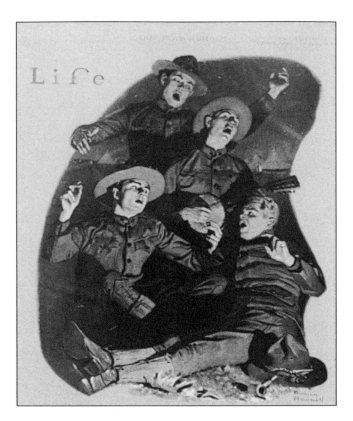

A Rockwell magazine cover from World War I.

In the First World War, colorful, smart posters with a direct and inspiring idea had helped whip up popular support and stimulate enlistment. As a young illustrator back then, Rockwell had painted a few war-related illustrations, even while he was serving in the navy.

For four months, he had been stationed on shore near Charleston, South Carolina, mainly employed in painting portraits of officers and their wives. He never saw action, though he was more than willing to go overseas. During this time, he was permitted to keep on painting covers for the *Post*, which he had begun to do in 1916, and for other magazines. For the most part, they were sentimental scenes of happy soldiers who looked more like well-scrubbed scouts on bivouac.

"I had done pictures of the doughboys in France, but it had all been fakery . . . dressing the models in costume — soldiers' uniforms."

For this new war, however, Rockwell already had painted a grim poster of a G.I. in a tattered uniform, firing a machine gun and running out of ammunition. "Let's Give Him Enough and On Time," the poster slogan read.

There was no false sentiment here, because that very spring thousands of Americans had fought to the end at Bataan and Corregidor in the Philippines. This stalwart machine gunner could have been one of them. For Norman Rockwell, there would be no more war images of idealized, carefree boys in uniform singing happily around a campfire.

Lately Rockwell often focused on Willie Gillis, the fictional G.I. he had created. Willie was the prototype of the average American boy in the army and absorbed by the mundane, ordinary life of a soldier in training. Over the course of the war, Willie would appear in realistic settings: peeling potatoes, collecting the mail, sitting in the servicemen's chapel, happily sleeping in his own bed while on leave, reading the hometown papers, and dreaming about girls.

By July 1942, good-natured Willie Gillis was as famous as Norman Rockwell, though only six *Post* covers old. For years people had often described each other in terms of characters in Rockwell pictures, and now young soldiers were being compared to Willie Gillis. Rockwell knew enough about the enlisted man's life away from the front so that Willie was real to everyone. Ordinary but resolute, Willie brought a sense of decency to the dirty business of warmaking. He was so popular that 2,500 enlarged reproductions of each Gillis *Post* cover were distributed, to be displayed wherever American troops were stationed.

Some of the national anxiety that surfaced in wartime was gently eased by the sight of Pvt. Willie Gillis, the citizen soldier with a quiet strength and determined, without show, to defend his country. To a nation engulfed in a war it was far from winning, Rockwell had already made a great contribution with Willie. About the illustrator, many a writer to the *Post* said simply, "He understands us."

Willie Gillis covers were fairly simple for Rockwell to do. The hardest part of painting, he always said, was thinking up good ideas, a daunting and agonizing task when good ideas did not come. With a war on, that had all changed, and new picture concepts were "dropping from the trees" because the whole country could identify with the same images. (In the

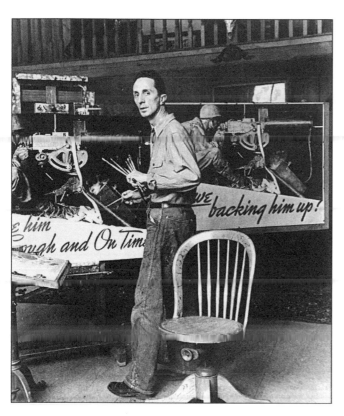

Increasing weapons production was a priority as the United States entered the war. Rockwell's first idea for the *Give Him Enough* poster was of a soldier at his gun waving to the viewer; the final version showed a determined gunner down to his last bullet.

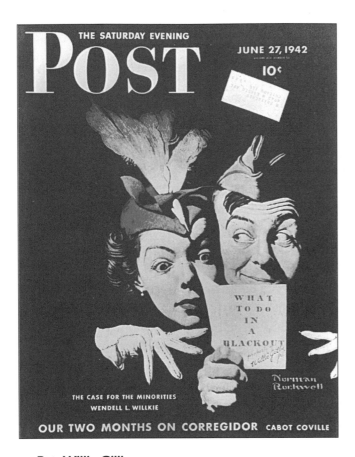

Pvt. Willie Gillis
appeared on the first
Post cover by Rockwell
in the new format
introduced by editor
Ben Hibbs.

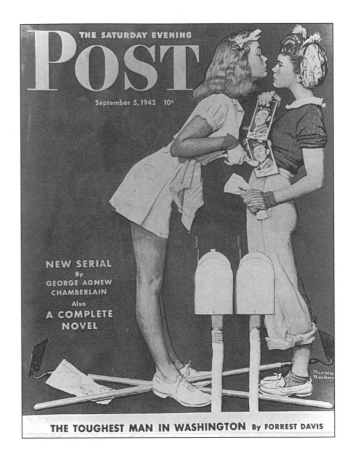

Lee and Patty Schaeffer,
daughters of *Post*
illustrator and
Arlington resident
Mead Schaeffer, posed
as rival girlfriends of
Willie Gillis.

later years of the war, Rockwell's ideas would include a mine worker wearing two stars to show he has two sons in the service; a visit to the president's busy White House office; supporting the war effort by selling war bonds; romance in the swirl of a crowded train station; soldiers wearily traveling by troop train; and of course the young G.I. coming home. Also, there were sober scenes that became subjects for Rockwell, such as returning wounded and Europeans suffering through bombing.)

Rockwell said: "Men go off to war; women go to work; draft boards, rationing boards, bond drives; soldiers abroad. . . ." He added, "That was what I knew about and what I painted best."

Extremely important to him were the new vigor and originality coming into his work as a result of painting the people and settings to be found near Arlington. The friends and neighbors who often served as subjects brought a freshness to Rockwell's painting, largely because they were not professionals acting out a role, as were so many of his models in New Rochelle.

"Now my pictures grew out of the world around me, the everyday life of my neighbors. I didn't fake anymore."

He found interesting models at town meetings, in stores, the post office, passing on the street, and at social events: he met Willie Gillis model Bob Buck at a square dance in the West Arlington Grange. Arlington's other two famous *Post* artists — Mead Schaeffer and Jack Atherton — and their families, also served as models for Rockwell. (Schaeffer's pretty daughters were depicted as rivals for the affection of Willie Gillis.)

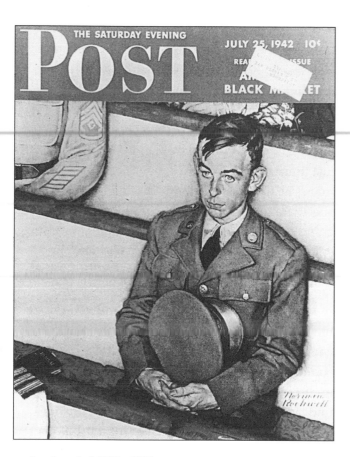

In church, Willie Gillis contemplates the seriousness of war and of his service to his country.

At this time, Rockwell's paintings became more realistic, his subjects being the down-to-earth, strong, and optimistic people he met every day. In the summer of 1942, America was in need of such strength and optimism as Norman Rockwell could give them.

One night in July, Rockwell lay half asleep, thinking about the four freedoms, "tossing in bed, mulling over the proclamation and the war, rejecting one idea after another and getting more and more discouraged as the minutes ticked by, empty and dark."

There was other stress in Rockwell's life just then: After twenty-six years as a *Post* "cover man," he had heard rumors that led him to speculate that the magazine was in danger of going out of business.

"The *Post* meant a great deal to me," he wrote, adding, "It was the only outlet, really, for the kind of work I liked to do best."

All his career Rockwell had counted on the income and the artistic opportunity the *Post* gave him. Now it looked to him as if it were coming to an end. Well, maybe it was a blessing in disguise, he thought: after all, he had been under constant pressure to create cover illustrations year after year, and perhaps as a result his "work was slipping."

At first, he wrote, he "was relieved" when he "imagined that the *Post* was about to go under. The loyalties of twenty-six years, the drive inside me to excel, my strong sense of competition, would never have permitted me to stop painting *Post* covers. But now the ship was going down and I would go down with it. There was something noble and easy about it."

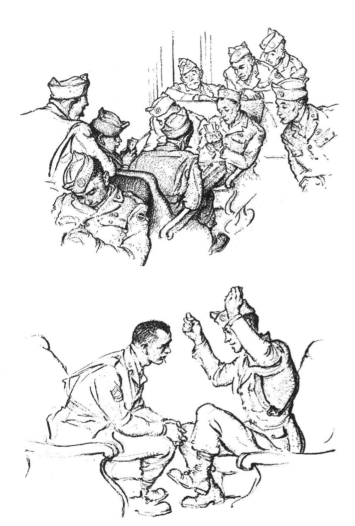

TELLING ABOUT HIS FIRST JUMP

Rockwell spent a night on a troop train, and in a series of sketches captured scenes from a soldier's life.

Even if the *Post* were to survive, Rockwell questioned whether different cover artists who were "more modern" might soon be brought in — new talent that would make it very plain that Norman Rockwell was simply too old-fashioned, out of date as well as out of ideas.

Ideas were the key to everything; ideas that could be brought to life in characters who were vivid, in paintings that told stories without words.

"Forget yourself," Rockwell's teachers had told him. "Step over the frame and live in the picture."

Living in the picture. Real people living the four freedoms. Freedom of speech. Men speaking out.

Suddenly he sat straight up in bed, remembering the recent town meeting when Jim Edgerton had stood up and spoken against a popular plan for building the new school. No one in the room had agreed with him, but they had let him speak.

"My gosh, I thought, that's it. There it is. Freedom of Speech."

Excited, Rockwell leaped from bed, eager to tell Mead Schaeffer that the first image of the four freedoms had been revealed at last. He made for the phone, thinking, "I'll illustrate the Four Freedoms using my Vermont neighbors as models. I'll express the ideas in simple, everyday scenes."

The abstract concepts of liberty would be painted in an American context — the very context Americans were fighting to defend. All the basic freedoms would be depicted just as they were lived, experienced, and at the same time learned.

These were no longer high-flown phrases and lofty platitudes, but real settings with real people, flesh and blood depictions of why Americans were fighting this war.

"Freedom of Speech — a New England town meeting. Freedom from Want — a Thanksgiving dinner." Rockwell had finally found the concept he wanted, but even more important: "I knew it was the best idea I'd ever had."

Abruptly realizing it was three o'clock in the morning, Rockwell decided not to telephone Schaeffer, because it would

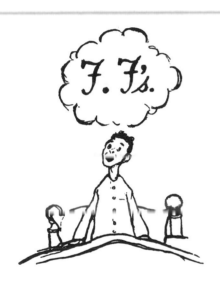

Rockwell sketched this image of himself inspired by his early morning "Four Freedoms" idea.

awaken the man's whole family as well as the others on the party line. Instead, he quickly dressed and rode his bicycle through the darkness to Schaeffer's house. He woke his friend, who — as he expected — immediately became as enthusiastic as Rockwell.

Acquainted from the years when both lived in New Rochelle, the two illustrators had become close since having moved to Arlington. (The Schaeffers arrived in 1940, just after the Rockwells moved in full-time.) They had great respect for each other, and often consulted, though their styles were very different — Schaeffer worked more from imagination, and in broader brush strokes, usually with less detail than Rockwell painted.

Schaeffer's confirmation that the four freedoms concept was exactly right made Rockwell all the more eager to get started, and he was at his easel by five o'clock that morning.

For *Freedom from Fear*, Rockwell used an idea that had been in his mind since he had first learned about the bombing attacks on Britain, in 1940: he depicted parents tucking in their sleeping children. It was an ordinary scene that Americans could take for granted, but when considered with the war headlines seen in the father's newspaper, this fleeting moment took on a larger meaning.

Freedom of Worship began as another everyday American scene, one that might not be likely in some other countries: several men of different races and religions enjoy a moment of idle banter in a country barbershop. Again, Rockwell envisioned a common moment, but one of profound significance — an expression of acceptance of other faiths and backgrounds, signifying American liberty to worship freely.

In the next few days, Schaeffer often looked in as Rockwell worked, offering encouragement and advice for the rough sketches. Rockwell was interested in what others thought about a painting in progress, especially wanting to know their first impressions and whether they caught on to the story he was telling. He always listened politely, though he did not always take advice, not even from the expert Schaeffer. According to Schaeffer, Rockwell liked to talk about a work in progress, largely to hear himself speak about it as a way of thinking through the ideas.

After a couple of days the preliminary work on the freedoms had gone very well, and Rockwell had four full-size (four feet by three feet) color sketches ready. Full-size color sketches were unusual for Rockwell, who normally showed his editors small-scale roughs, often only in pencil. Now, however, he wanted everything to go just right in Washington, and he intended to be as persuasive as possible. He was sure what the government wanted, and full-size sketches would make it easier for bureaucrats to see what he intended to paint.

Excited and full of confidence, Rockwell rolled up the sketches and, along with Schaeffer (who had a set of poster ideas, himself), took the train for Washington These were two of the most important and well known illustrators in the country, carrying fresh and hard-won new ideas to lift the spirits of the nation at war. Moreover, they both intended to work for the war effort free of charge.

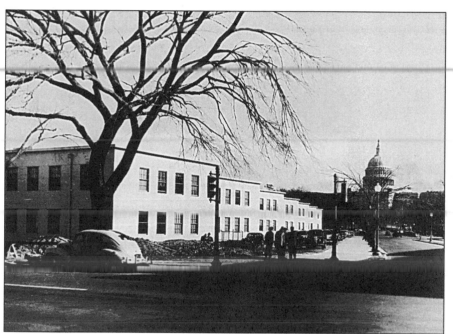

When Rockwell and Mead Schaeffer visited Washington, D.C., they found numerous new agencies and temporary buildings created by the war effort, such as these along the Mall in front of the Capitol.

As the train passed through Philadelphia on the track to Washington, D.C., Rockwell might have been thinking about a meeting he had arranged with the *Saturday Evening Post* at the magazine's offices there. He was to stop off in Philadelphia on the way back from Washington and meet with the new editor, Ben Hibbs. Rockwell had no idea what to expect from Hibbs, but was not certain the man would last as editor.

From 1898 until 1936, the *Post*'s domineering but brilliant editor, George Horace Lorimer, had run the *Post* with an iron hand. Lorimer's uncanny sense of what readers wanted had built the *Post* into the most influential magazine in the country.

"It was *his* magazine, his alone," Rockwell wrote. "He made the final decision on every story, okayed every cover. . . . And he thought the *Post* was the greatest magazine ever published."

Over the years, Rockwell learned just how to work his favorite ideas by Lorimer, making cover presentations by acting out the story in the painting. No matter how many ideas were offered, Lorimer would accept only three. So Rockwell would present five ideas, enthusiastically acting out the three he wanted Lorimer to take, and only halfheartedly portraying the other two. Lorimer invariably accepted the right three and rejected the other two in accordance with the warmth of Rockwell's performance.

In 1936, health failing, Lorimer reluctantly resigned, and things at the *Post* were not the same. For five years after Lorimer retired, Rockwell had worked for the next editor, Wesley W. Stout, and his relationship with the *Post* had become unpleasantly difficult. With Lorimer, Rockwell had always known whether or not the editor liked a cover. With Stout, however, Rockwell seldom could tell what the editor thought; invariably, with every new painting, Rockwell was asked to make some annoying little change — down to the color of shoes.

Rockwell came to expect these niggling objections from Stout, annoying changes that "sapped my inspiration" and "made me unsure of myself." Further, he was tired of having to prove himself anew with every *Post* cover. Now things had suddenly been altered again, with the unknown Ben Hibbs replacing Stout.

That spring, Rockwell had met Hibbs for the first time and had gone home unsure about the soundness of the man's judgment. He told Mary he liked the new editor, but did not think Hibbs would be successful, especially because "he accepted all my sketches, *all nine*. He didn't turn down one. It's wonderful, but . . . you can't run a magazine that way."

The fact was that Rockwell had worked hard to create all nine sketches, wanting them to be his very best, because if he had followed his usual practice with Lorimer and included a few "bad ideas" for Hibbs, "he might reject the whole batch and I'd be off the *Post*. Believe me, I put everything I had into those nine sketches."

In the same way, but for nobler reasons, he had put his all into the sketches for Roosevelt's four freedoms.

If Rockwell and Schaeffer read the newspapers as their train clattered out of Philadelphia toward Washington, they would have found dismal war news: the Japanese were still advancing, having seized more strategic islands in the Pacific, and invading New Guinea, dangerously close to Australia. On the high seas the war was threatening to become a disaster for the Allies, especially in the North Atlantic, where American convoys to Britain were suffering heavy losses to enemy U-boats.

In the past few weeks the German Afrika Korps had driven the British Eighth Army back across the Egyptian desert, and it seemed the vital Suez Canal might soon be lost to the Allies. In Russia, German tanks had captured the rich oil fields of the Caucasus and were pushing aggressively eastward to the city of Stalingrad. For the Allies, this was one of the lowest points in the war, and it was up to the United States to be that arsenal of democracy before it was too late.

The printing of posters and brochures was a vital part of this vast American war effort. Posters were meant to stimulate factory production of war matériel and to rally and inform the people. The four freedoms ideals were key to the government's overall propaganda program to inspire the people, but there were many other more mundane — yet also important — concepts in need of publicizing.

According to a 1942 article in the magazine *American Artist*, "The artist, through the dramatic appeal of his posters, becomes the government's mouthpiece in a language every citizen can understand."

One notably successful public information campaign, according to the Office of War Information (OWI), was for recycling valuable materials: "The tonnage of rubber and metals salvaged directly as a consequence of the graphic artists' work . . . is certainly vast," said an OWI spokesman in a published letter to *American Artist*.

In various periodicals, artists and illustrators were given detailed advice about which topics would evoke a positive response from the general public when it came to supporting the war effort. Among these were patriotism; nobility and dignity; liberty, democracy, and freedom; idealism; pride; anger, fear, and hate (try to avoid this one, it was said); war production; and also humor.

Also of utmost importance was the sale of war bonds — and the use of posters to stimulate those sales. In a newsreel speech early that spring, President Roosevelt announced he wanted to bring in the enormous sum of $1 billion a month from war bond sales in every community in the country. Voluntary nationwide support of the war effort — whether financial or through personal effort — was absolutely essential to victory. Thus, many a Washington bureaucrat's career hinged on his ability to produce effective printed propaganda to accomplish some war-related task.

At the same time, feelings in the writers' division of OWI ran strongly for publishing only the truth. Staff members flatly objected to any publicity campaign designed to "sell" the war effort the way toothpaste or cola was marketed. There were some big-name volunteers from the advertising world on government advisory councils, but so far most "education" agencies such as OWI were run by men who took pride in resisting hype or misrepresentation.

"Tell the truth and nothing but the truth," said OWI head Elmer Davis, a former broadcast executive; he added, "The truth is on our side."

Yet, there was no doubt that the purpose of OWI was to inspire right-thinking and acceptable forms of behavior that would promote and contribute to the war effort. Advertising and motion-picture executives were beginning to come to power in OWI, and the days were numbered for literate programs that published thoughtful analyses of war subjects for a thinking public. Controversies were brewing between writers who were at pains to explain the serious side of the war and those, such as the film executives, whose productions too often were escapist and delusive when it came to handling important issues at the root of the worldwide conflict.

When Rockwell and Schaeffer arrived in Washington, every government agency was grinding along at a furious pace and most officials were overworked. Bureaucrats were under tremendous pressure to perform, and at the same time were trying to fend off the pervasive gloom of recent bad war news.

Before coming to Washington the two illustrators had arranged to meet Orion Wynford, head of the creative department at Brown & Bigelow, publishers of Rockwell's Boy Scout calendars. Well known in government circles, Wynford had eagerly offered to introduce Rockwell and Schaeffer to all the right people at the various agencies. Wynford met them at the hotel, "his white suit and swelling mane of white hair sparkling in the sun."

Recalling that trip to Washington in his autobiography, Rockwell wrote:

> We set out the next morning. As we entered the first office the secretary jumped up. "Oh, Mr. Wynford," she said, "thank you so much for the lovely bouquet of roses. And the candy was delicious." Orion smiled and made a deprecatory gesture. At the door of the second office we visited the security guard said, "Swell party, Mr. Wynford. Go right in. *You* don't have to be checked." Evidently Orion had oiled the works.
>
> But, just as evidently, the oil had not penetrated beyond the anterooms. None of the government officials could help us. The war was going badly; nobody had time for posters. Robert Patterson, the Undersecretary of War, said, "We'd love to print your Four Freedoms, but we can't. I'm sorry. We just don't have the time to spare to arrange it. We think they'd be a fine contribution. We'd be delighted if *someone* would publish them."
>
> Schaef and I became more and more discouraged as we were turned down by one official after another. After a while even Orion became rather subdued. Not because our posters weren't being accepted but because his weren't. He was trying to drum up business for Brown and Bigelow. He had a portfolio full of sketches which his company's calendar artists had done. For instance, a beautiful girl leaning forward, bosoms rampant, captioned: Will YOU help?

That was all right. Schaef and I didn't mind if he stropped his own razor while showing us around. But he kept interrupting us. Schaef and I would no more than begin to exhibit our work and explain that we didn't want to be paid for anything, we just wanted to do something for the war effort, than Orion would pull a girly poster from his portfolio and, laying it on the desk in front of the official, say: "Mr. Sec-re-tary. I have here a poster calculated to stir, to inspire, *pride* of country in every American breast. We ask no more than the paper to print it on." And he'd continue in this vein, displaying one poster after another, until the Secretary ushered us out of his office, pleading urgent business. So Schaef and I never got to tell our story.

But I doubt whether it would have made any difference. Once Orion excused himself for a minute and we almost jumped on the army colonel in whose office we were at the moment. "We don't want money," we said. "Just let us do our posters." But, no, the colonel was sympathetic but hopeless; he couldn't arrange it.

Finally, late in the afternoon, we found ourselves in the Office of War Information (or, to speak plainly, the propaganda department). I showed the Four Freedoms to the man in charge of posters but he wasn't even interested. "The last war, you illustrators did the posters," he said. "This war we're going to use fine arts men, real artists. If you want to make a contribution to the war effort you can do some of these pen-and-ink drawings for the Marine Corps calisthenics manual. But as far as your Four Freedoms go, we aren't interested."

"Well, I don't know," I said, leafing through the layouts of the calisthenics manual (you know, simple drawings of men arms up, arms out, arms to the side), and remembering what high hopes I'd had when I conceived the Four Freedoms, "I guess not."

And Schaef, Orion and I left the office and went back to the hotel. That was the final blow. Schaef and I decided to give up trying to interest people in our posters and my Four Freedoms. The next morning, depressed and discouraged, we took the train back to New York.

Before going to New York, however, Rockwell had to stop off in Philadelphia for that appointment with Ben Hibbs at the *Post*.

After all those years with George Horace Lorimer, it was strange enough for Rockwell to call the revered editor of the *Post* by his first name, as Ben Hibbs wanted him to do. It was also unsettling to be in Lorimer's former office, with the same pictures and upholstered armchairs, the familiar high ceilings and paneled walls. And behind the desk were those large, bright windows which used to silhouette Lorimer whenever he rose to greet visitors. He was an impressive, old-fashioned gentleman who continually paced the floor, heels thudding, whenever Rockwell made a cover proposal.

Now, instead of the overbearing Lorimer striding toward Rockwell with those piercing eyes and "his big hand thrust out to me," the artist was met by a "tall, lanky man with a serious, comfortable face." Ben Hibbs, a midwesterner and "rather young," even sat back with his feet up on the long, polished conference table — and he was in shirtsleeves, no less. Rockwell had to admit that Hibbs had already shown daring, having redesigned the venerable cover of the magazine, blowing up the word "Post" and putting it in the upper left corner. The circle that always had surrounded the cover art was gone, for better or worse.

Rockwell had received letters about the new format. "The world is breaking apart, they said . . . and now the *Post* has been changed."

Still, Rockwell told himself, few editors of struggling magazines would have the courage to make such a drastic alteration — even though it might be needed. He gave Ben Hibbs credit for that.

In the meeting with Hibbs, Rockwell discussed several ideas for future covers and inside illustrations. Understandably, Rockwell had little enthusiasm and spunk left after his disappointment in Washington. During the course of the conversation, he offhandedly mentioned his two days at the capital, and Hibbs asked why he had been there. Rockwell casually told him that he and Schaeffer were offering their services to the government, but that there had been no interest in his four freedoms series. Hibbs asked to see what Rockwell had offered. Rockwell "hauled the sketches out and showed them to him, explaining rather listlessly what they were all about, what I'd been trying to do."

Hibbs listened intently, then interrupted, clearly excited: "Norman, you've got to do them for us."

Startled, Rockwell collected himself before replying, "I'd be delighted to."

"Well, drop everything else," said Hibbs, insisting that Rockwell work only on the four freedoms and not paint any covers or illustrations until he was finished.

Rockwell was wondering why he had not thought of the *Post* for the paintings of the four freedoms before this. Obviously, being so bluntly and unexpectedly turned down in Washington had thrown him until now.

Hibbs asked how long the work would take. Rockwell's excitement was mounting as he estimated he would need no more than two months. It was all quickly agreed upon.

Rockwell wasted no time, immediately hurrying back to Arlington, "rejuvenated, and set right to work."

Part Two

Norman Rockwell's Four Freedoms

Rockwell with *Freedom of Speech*, inspired by a New England town meeting.

From the front of his white colonial house, Norman Rockwell could look across the Batten Kill, with the sunlight sparkling on the river's surface, and see an island where the only local killing had occurred during the American Revolution.

Rockwell visualized that scene from time to time: a young man had been shot by the doctor who had owned the house across the river — shot while stealing cattle to feed the "Green Mountain Boys," a band of Vermont rebels under the command of Ethan Allen. Before going off to join the rebels, the lad had been the doctor's apprentice.

In his mind, Rockwell could hear the rifle go off, see the apprentice falling into the water and "the doctor, aghast at what he'd done, splashing over to the island and picking the boy up, yelling for his wife."

American history was alive for Rockwell, who had researched and illustrated many scenes from the past. Like the great illustrators he admired — especially Howard Pyle — Rockwell had to know everything about his subject: character and personality, and the things his subject would wear or use. In Rockwell's studio was a large collection of antiques, uniforms, old guns, swords, artifacts, and a file of old prints and images — kept as props and gathered over the twenty-eight years of his career.

In 1938, when first considering whether to buy the colonial farmhouse with its broad fields, two red barns, and apple orchard, Rockwell had found the Revolutionary War story to be part of its charm. By 1942, however, the house felt lonely, being half a mile from the nearest neighbor. There were times when Rockwell considered the turning out of the last light at night much like "pulling a black bag over your head," it was so dark.

The solitude of the historic house on the Batten Kill gave Rockwell peace and quiet to work undisturbed, but there were drawbacks. For all the beauty of their home's rustic setting above the river, its remoteness was not easy for the family, especially for Mary Rockwell, who had been raised in suburban Alhambra next to Los Angeles, and had lived with Rockwell in the affluent suburbs of New York. Their three sons — Jarvis ("Jerry"), eleven; Tommy, nine; and Peter, six — were for the most part still finding their ways as transplanted suburban New York boys in a rural setting. Jarvis in particular was none too happy about being uprooted from bustling New Rochelle.

Mary had to handle most of the upbringing of the boys while her husband spent long hours in the studio. Though she had a married couple for help with the house and garden, there was much for her to do, both for the family and in managing the business side of Rockwell's career. Mary was always busy, carrying out the endless chores of a mother of three who was involved in the life of a famous illustrator. It helped that the native Vermonters were fond of her, and she was well known in the village, seen daily running about in the family's wood-sided Ford station wagon.

Just before he married Mary in 1930, Rockwell had been under tremendous pressure, both professionally and emotionally. For a year after his divorce from his first wife, Irene O'Connor — who after fourteen years of marriage was still uninterested in his art and was something of an aspiring socialite — he endured a lonely, "rootless" existence in New York. When he went to California and met Mary Barstow, a Stanford-educated schoolteacher, their marriage "rescued" him, he said.

Mary was her husband's first audience, often called over to the studio "to look at the picture" in progress. She loved his work and, as he painted, often sat for hours reading aloud to him. Their favorites were Tolstoy (*War and Peace* twice over) and Dickens, sometimes Henry James, Jane Austen, and Voltaire. It also was good for the Rockwells that so many artists lived between Bennington, sixteen miles to the south, and Manchester, eight miles to the north.

Their friends, Elizabeth and Mead Schaeffer, who lived with two teenage daughters a few miles away on a back road, shared many of the same day-to-day experiences with the Rockwells. When they got together they talked about pictures for *Post* covers just as they did about their children. Rockwell convinced them all to join the West Arlington Grange, where they sometimes went square dancing: Rockwell was especially good at it, though some of the farm girls could whirl the reedy artist off his feet when the music got lively.

All through the summer of 1942, Norman Rockwell was completely wrapped up in the *Four Freedoms*, but the work did not go well, and it became apparent that his promise to finish the paintings in two months was unrealistic.

Right from the start, he struggled with *Freedom of Speech*, although he was satisfied with his model: gas station owner Carl Hess "had a noble head," according to Gene Pelham, the artist's photographer, who originally had suggested Hess. *Freedom of Worship*, too, was as yet an uncertain image, but the other two — *Freedom from Want* and *Freedom from Fear* — were fairly well conceptualized and would be painted last.

That summer, there were visits to the studio from other illustrators and commercial artists, including John Cullen Murphy, a former boy-model for Rockwell in New Rochelle and already an accomplished young illustrator. Serving in the army, Murphy was on leave when he came up to see Rockwell, who years before had taken him under his wing to teach him illustration and had been instrumental in persuading his parents to send him to art school.

A year or so earlier, Murphy had been working on a painting of an enlisted man holding a package from home while other soldiers loomed above him, eager to see what goodies it contained. Murphy, who was in the army at the time, was startled to get a call from Rockwell, who said he had heard about the painting. Rockwell told him that coincidentally the first Willie Gillis illustration of the same subject was soon to come out as a *Post* cover. Murphy agreed to forgo the painting, and shortly afterwards received his own food package chock-full of delicacies, courtesy of the Rockwells.

When visiting the Arlington studio, Murphy saw the color sketches of the *Four Freedoms* and was struck by how unusually enthusiastic Rockwell was about this work. Though Rockwell was always deeply absorbed by whatever painting was underway — almost every one started out in his mind to become his masterpiece — Murphy had never known him to be so excited about an idea.

Gene Pelham was there photographing models the day Murphy visited. Rockwell asked Murphy, who was in uniform, to pose standing behind a table and be photographed for several perspectives to help with the composition of *Freedom of Speech*. Later that evening Murphy went out to dinner with the Rockwells. As was typical for Rockwell, it was not until the very last minute that he stopped work and came out of the studio to go to the restaurant. Also typical was Rockwell's interest in being part of the Arlington community; he had to leave dinner early to take his turn at the responsibilities of an air raid warden. Jim Edgerton, who lived in the hamlet of West Arlington, was building a structure for airplane spotters, and there were a number of civil defense drills to be practiced.

In late October, another visitor was Joseph Busciglio, a nineteen-year-old artist from Florida, who had traveled by bus to Arlington all the way from Baltimore. Walking the last few miles from the bus station to the studio, Busciglio arrived when Rockwell was working on a head for the first version of *Worship*, the barbershop scene. Rockwell had two easels set up, one with the charcoal version and the other with the oil painting that was underway. Some *Life* magazine tear sheets showing several examples of heads were on a table off to the side; in a corner of the studio was the completed final version of *Freedom of Speech*, in a white baroque frame.

Rockwell was in some hurry to make progress on *Worship*, saying the *Post* editor was coming up next week. He was also hard at work on the magazine's Christmas cover at the time. Despite his demanding schedule, Rockwell let young Busciglio stay at the studio for two hours, and gave him a charcoal of one of the Willie Gillis series as a gift.

During these war years, the Vermont landscape and its people came to epitomize, in the popular mind, a seclusion and security from the outside world, as if still existing in the good old days. New Englanders were characterized as sensible, self-reliant, fair-minded, and taciturn, and the countryside idealized. Rural New England was widely admired, whether in the sophisticated yet plain poetry of Vermont's Robert Frost, four-time winner of the Pulitzer Prize, or in the sentimental portrayals of the mass media, as far from battlefronts and bombs, from churning factories and teeming, dirty cities.

Certainly, this image of Vermont was part of the appeal to Rockwell and other recent transplants to the region. In turn, Rockwell's depictions of his neighbors — salt-of-the-earth people who did not have to act to portray ordinary Americans — appearing around the country in millions of magazine covers, advertisements, and illustrations, had contributed greatly to this image of Vermont as the archetype of what was good about America.

As it was, Rockwell's illustrations always had been timely. More than ever these days, his work had that exacting detail and realism most people now wanted to see, while still depicting broadly recognizable characters. Rockwell's work appealed more than ever to the majority of Americans.

Also appealing to that same popular taste were the music business and the movies, which had singled out New England, and Vermont in particular, as a quiet and peaceful place to escape the noisy rise of Fascism and Communism, the anxiety of war, and the shadow of the passing Depression (though in reality Vermont's agricultural areas had been hard hit, and poverty was still evident).

It was in 1942 that Irving Berlin's "White Christmas" was first sung by Bing Crosby in the film *Holiday Inn*, set at a ski lodge in New England. For the past ten years entrepreneurs had been building ski resorts in New England's hills and mountains, and new myths spoke of snowy fields and cozy fire-places. *Holiday Inn* was the first of many cheery, patriotic musicals created for Americans in the midst of total world war. The song "White Christmas" won the Academy Award, and two years later the hit song "Moonlight in Vermont" would use the same themes, which reminded men and women, stationed all over the world, of home.

In this way, Americans were offered a refuge, even if only in the minds of readers and listeners and movie-goers who might never get to Vermont. Yet, for all the myth-making, it seemed to Norman Rockwell that rural New Englanders were, indeed, living out the four essential freedoms in the ordinary activities of their daily lives. At the same time, their fathers, husbands, brothers, and sons were in the service defending those freedoms — freedoms which President Roosevelt now called upon the new alliance of "United Nations" to guarantee all people, everywhere in the world.

In August, 1942, a long pamphlet entitled "The United Nations Fight for the Four Freedoms" was produced by the Office of War Information's (OWI) Domestic Branch. The project was under the direction of nationally known poet Archibald MacLeish, the Librarian of Congress. The scholarly MacLeish had fashioned the copywriting division of the Domestic Branch in his own mold, liberal and brainy. Subtitled "The Rights of All Men — Everywhere," the pamphlet was sixteen dense pages and opened with a brisk introduction by Roosevelt, who said, "The four freedoms of common humanity are as much elements of man's needs as air and sunlight."

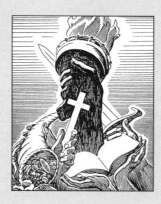

The United Nations fight for the

Four Freedoms

The Rights of All Men—Everywhere

The pamphlet "The United Nations Fight for the Four Freedoms" was produced by the Office of War Information in August 1942.

Right from its first sentence, the main text of the pamphlet looked to the future: "Beyond the war lies the peace." Its stated objective was to examine and clearly define the four essential freedoms, adding that "To talk of war aims, shouting over the din of battle while the planet rocks and vibrates, may seem futile to some. Yet the talk must go on among free peoples. The faith people have in themselves is what the free have to build upon."

In his introduction, Roosevelt said these freedoms are the heritage of every creed and every race, a heritage too often "long withheld" from many. He wrote, "We of the United Nations have the power and the men and the will at last to assure man's heritage."

Quoted in full is the United Nations declaration of New Year's Day, 1942, which pledged twenty-six countries to fight on, none to make a separate peace with the enemy until "Hitlerism" was defeated. The goal of peace was to guarantee the four essential freedoms as the founding principles of a new international order. Although the military alliance known as the United Nations was not yet functioning like the subsequent United Nations organization established in 1945, the pamphlet envisioned such a development:

"The United Nations, now engaged in a common cause . . . plan a world in which men stand straight and walk free. . . . This free-ness, this liberty, this precious thing men love and mean to save, is the good granite ledge on which the United Nations now propose to raise their new world after victory."

At the end of World War I, Roosevelt had joined President Woodrow Wilson's crusade to bring the United States into the newly formed League of Nations. Through this membership, Wilson wanted America to defend and advance democracy around the world, but an isolationist Congress declined to participate in the League. When Wilson succumbed to a stroke in 1919, it was Roosevelt who became the standard-bearer for this unsuccessful attempt to bring the United States into the League. Now, more than two decades after Wilson's defeat, the new United Nations alliance might be transformed by American leadership into a more powerful world organization with even loftier goals than the original League, which had collapsed in impotence before World War II began.

The OWI pamphlet had no byline, but it bore the stamp of MacLeish's idealism and Roosevelt's own firmly held beliefs when it stated, "The declaration of the four freedoms . . . is not a promise of a gift, which, under certain conditions, the people will receive; it is a declaration of a design which the people themselves may execute."

In 1942, the widespread publicity about the importance of the four freedoms led to discussions about them in such diverse publications as *Education* ("Contributions of the English to the Four Freedoms"), *Catholic World* ("United States Peace Aims"), *Annals of the American Academy* ("Symbols of National Solidarity: the Four Freedoms") and *Parents' Magazine* ("Cultivating the Four Freedoms: Children Must Learn Their Meaning at Home").

The American arts community assisted in the campaign to keep war aims in the public mind, with *The Freedoms Conquer* (above) by William Soles, and *The Four Freedoms* (opposite) by Ralph Fabri.

In the *Parents' Magazine* article, written by educator Dr. Frank Kingdon, it was observed that unchecked personal "intolerances" of many parents do great harm to their children: "The four freedoms will have little meaning for anyone who is not convinced of the inherent dignity of every human being of every race, color and creed."

The four freedoms ideals also became a theme for "Artists for Victory," a consortium of twenty-one artists' groups, including the Society of Illustrators, of which Rockwell was a prominent

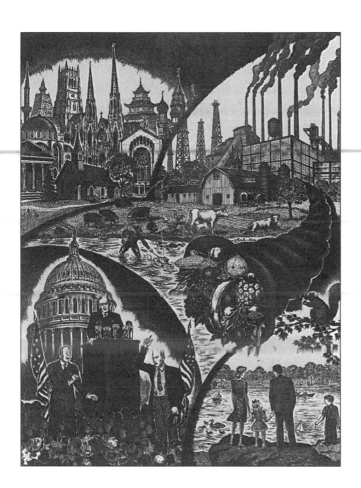

member. This and other professional artists' organizations helped fulfill requests from government agencies for artwork that promoted and publicized the war effort.

Artists for Victory aimed "to render effective the talents and abilities of artists in the prosecution of World War II and the protection of this country." It took Roosevelt's Four Freedoms speech of January, 1941, as a basis of its philosophy and pledged a minimum of five million hours of work from American artists. The organization started its own four freedoms campaign, which would lead up to celebrating the "Four Freedoms Days," designated for September 12-19, 1943.

Printmakers were called upon to submit works on the theme "America in the War," with one hundred to be chosen for exhibition in a number of separate but simultaneous shows across the country to open in October, 1943. The most prominent print in the show's promotion material — it was published by *Art News* in the contest's announcement — was a silkscreen by Richard Floethe entitled *The Liberator*, spelling out the four freedoms. Another, a woodcut by William Soles called *The Freedoms Conquer*, showed an American soldier bayonetting a Japanese. One was a collage-format etching by Ralph Fabri of several American domestic scenes, entitled *The Four Freedoms*.

For the most part modern in concept, and sometimes grotesque in their depiction of the enemy, these one hundred prints were a far cry from the work Norman Rockwell created. The show "America in the War" circulated for several years — sometimes in smaller versions — in USO centers and military bases, where their stark imagery contrasted with Willie Gillis posters.

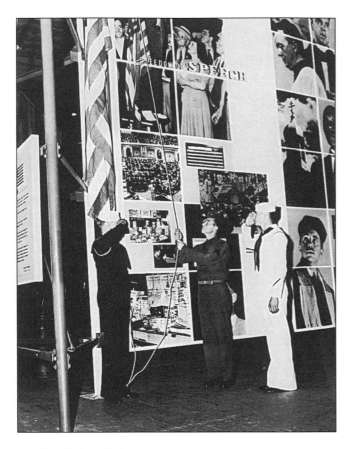

The Office of Emergency Management commissioned Jean Carlu to create a billboard-sized photomontage of the four freedoms in 1941; it was shown in Washington D.C., and New York City.

Artists for Victory also held a national war-poster competition to disseminate slogans prepared by OWI, and sponsored other exhibits on the theme of global peace after the war was won.

A number of artists already had been commissioned to depict the four freedoms. These included a postage stamp design, and a billboard-size photomontage by poster artist Jean Carlu commissioned by the Office of Emergency Management for display in Washington. The freedoms also were depicted on decorative panels which were to decorate the Washington offices of the United Nations, painted by Dutch artist Gerard Hordyke; and a large mural, twenty-two by eleven feet, was being painted by Hugo Ballin for the Burbank city hall, symbolically illustrating the freedoms by using images that ranged from Moses and the Ten Commandments to a woman shopping for food at the market.

Roosevelt himself asked sculptor Walter Russell to create a piece, since, as he said, "Through the medium of the arts a far greater number of people could be brought to understand the four freedoms." He suggested four angels with upraised, protecting wings, and facing the four points of the compass. Thus, Roosevelt and government agencies were both contributing to and benefiting from the enthusiasm for the four freedoms as being reasons for fighting the war. He and key advisor Treasury Secretary Henry Morgenthau, Jr., soon were to capitalize on that enthusiasm to encourage the buying of war bonds.

It was one thing to be willing to fight the war, but it also had to be financed. How was the United States to pay for the staggering cost of worldwide conflict? Increasing taxes or printing quantities of money were not desirable.

Congress fought new or higher taxes, and the dangers of inflation mitigated against a sudden wholesale enlargement of the money supply.

To raise cash, Roosevelt and Treasury Secretary Morgenthau were determined to sell billions of dollars worth of government bonds in small denominations to the general public. In addition to resisting the need for taxes and the pressures of inflation, selling these war bonds would also establish a large national savings base, thereby strengthening the economy. Those same savings also would be extremely valuable after the war, when the wartime boom subsided and there would be a threat of recession.

In order to sell vast quantities of war bonds to average American citizens throughout a period of years, Roosevelt and Morgenthau set a great promotional machine into action, known as "The Defense Savings Program." As part of the bond-sales campaign, the idea of fighting for human freedom became central to almost every government message exhorting the people to contribute to the national cause.

When it came to persuading Americans to buy bonds, much of the pitch depended on patriotism, everyone being called to do his or her part in the war effort. Writers and artists, film-makers and radio broadcasters worked together for the common purposes of not only lifting the spirits of the people and bolstering their resolve to fight on, but also to help finance the war.

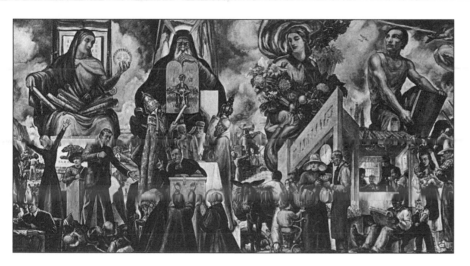

The City of Burbank, California, commissioned Hugo Ballin to paint a four freedoms mural for the new city hall building. Completed in 1942, the mural combined symbolic and realistic portrayals of the freedoms.

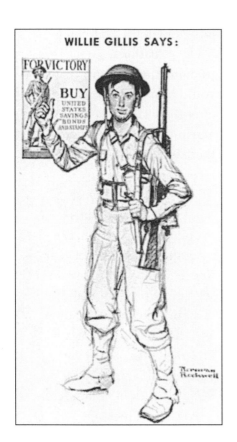

Rockwell joined his "Willie Gillis" character with the "Minuteman" symbol of the 1942 war bonds campaign.

The purchase of war bonds, however, was only one of many initiatives sought by the war effort and its attendant publicity: the calls for total mobilization also demanded increased production, victory gardens, and rubber and scrap metal drives. The clamor of these many messages threatened to confuse the public information about the aims of the war, especially the four freedoms ideals.

In November, 1942, MacLeish's OWI associate Henry Pringle attempted to develop a "war creed" or a "battle creed" to articulate clearly why the war was being fought. One version called upon Americans to fight for total victory "whatever it may cost in Blood and Treasure," and to aspire to a "World of the New Morning," when everyone may, thanks to "Justice, have an equal chance to share whatever the Good earth has to offer to her sons."

Another version, this one drafted by poet and novelist Steven Vincent Benét, was similar in spirit, and declared in its first line, "We, the people of the United States, believe that man was born free." Benét went on to say, "We cannot and will not live in a world ruled by tyrants. We cannot and will not pass on such a world to our children."

The people were exhorted to build a new world in part by the sacrifice of their "treasure." Roosevelt and Morgenthau counted on that willing sacrifice to finance the war, and they stressed the importance of payroll savings plans which took money directly out of wages for war-bond purchase. Morgenthau wanted to more than double the sale of war bonds to a billion dollars a month, and he established quotas for each state.

"Every community in this country will have to do its share to reach this quota," Morgenthau announced. "All of us who earn regular pay should set aside an average of at least ten per cent of it every week for buying War Bonds. . . . It's not only smart to be thrifty, but our future depends on it."

Such blunt emotional appeals to the public's sense of the practical succeeded well when used in tandem with hyped-up films and radio broadcasts that beat the drums of war. The OWI Domestic Branch writers and their more abstract, intellectual approach to explaining "why we fight" began to lose favor in government.

Increasingly, conflict developed in OWI between MacLeish's literary element with its progressive, liberal views, and the high-powered advertising specialists and movie-makers, who well understood how — in an emotional way — to sell public participation in the war effort.

Some radio appeals and war announcements were described by the Domestic Branch writers as "so phony and so hoked up that they stink violently," with "too Goddamned much cleverness, sleight of hand . . . and too Goddamned little straight talking over the table at an adult public."

Meanwhile, powerful conservative leaders in Congress loudly complained about the liberal Domestic Branch of OWI, some asserting that the division was no more than a mouthpiece for Roosevelt's New Deal policies. The conflict raged, with the result being the resignation of MacLeish and the rise to power of advertising and film promoters.

In Washington, a struggle raged to win the hearts, minds, and money of ordinary Americans, but as yet no single work of art had been found to portray the four essential freedoms as powerfully as had Roosevelt's speech in 1941.

Meanwhile, in Vermont, Norman Rockwell worked on, undergoing his own struggle — not for ordinary America's heart, mind, or money, but to find a picture of its soul.

Though he knew little about OWI or the inner workings of Morgenthau's war bonds campaign, Rockwell followed the war news, reading newspapers or magazines at breakfast and lunch, and sometimes listening to radio broadcasts while he worked. Until he found the right final image for a picture, however, or if working on a difficult aspect of the painting, he avoided all distractions in the studio, including the radio.

Rockwell once said many illustrators look for the most dominant or dramatic incident of a story and illustrate that. "I prefer to discover the atmosphere of a story — the feeling behind it — and then to express this basic quality."

In *Freedom of Speech*, the setting of the town meeting and the characters were clear in his mind, but the straight-ahead composition he had first chosen failed to satisfy him. He wanted to find the point of view that would make "a strong, precise statement," with just the right feeling behind it. After weeks of hard work, he thought the first *Freedom of Speech* painting was "too diverse, it went every which way and didn't settle anywhere or say anything."

By the time Rockwell worked out the final perspective — seen from a front bench, as if the viewer were turning and looking back up at the speaker — he had painted *Freedom of Speech* over on canvas four times. Twice he had almost finished it, with only a few days of work left when he had decided it was not right. The final version placed the emphasis on the speaker rather than on the assembly. Although the painting pleased Rockwell, it was only the first of the freedoms, and summer was already over.

As a rule the idea of Rockwell's subject was first developed with a rough pencil sketch followed by full-blown finished charcoal drawings. This was followed by a color sketch or two before he would put brush to canvas.

"Too many novices, I believe, wait until they are on the canvas before trying to solve many of their problems. It is much better to wrestle with them ahead of time through studies. . . . Such a practice saves time and insures a better job."

During Rockwell's final execution of a painting, he liked to ask a wide range of people for their reactions as he went along. Open-minded and self-critical, Rockwell in this way constantly probed both his own thinking and tested the clarity of the story behind the picture. As a young man in art school — at the National Academy of Design and the Art Students League, both in New York — Rockwell had been serious and meticulous, and considered so sober, hardworking, and responsible that other students called him "The Deacon." Still remaining from those years as an eager student determined to become a professional was his penchant for efficiency and organization in the studio.

Spacious and well-lit, Rockwell's Arlington studio had none of the stereotypical artist's clutter and spatter. His easel stood in the center of the main room, which had a cathedral ceiling. The studio was about twenty-four feet square, with a fireplace and a couple of comfortable chairs in front it. Most of the wall opposite the fireplace was a huge two-story window, facing the north light. A cushioned window seat was built in, and curtains screened the bottom level of the glass for privacy.

The studio's knotty pine walls were decorated with framed paintings and prints, and had bookshelves as well as several shelves with ship models, sculptures, and figurines. Hanging above doors and side windows were old swords and guns, and there was a mirror on one wall along with a chest of drawers, which held newspaper and magazine clippings, fan mail, and reference materials as well as some .22 caliber bullets and shotgun shells, kept handy for target shooting with the boys. In the studio were resource books, busts, a cluster of valued pipes, walking sticks he had carved himself, a few animal skulls, some treasured Howard Pyle prints, and a favorite old pewter mug.

Rockwell's working place was always kept immaculate; he frequently "neatened up," sometimes as a way of relaxing if he felt himself becoming tight or losing his perspective. (The older he became, he once said, the more he seemed to clean up instead of paint; he expected that one day he would only clean up.) Rolls of canvas, extra tools, and framing materials were stored away in the workroom beneath the balcony, where there was also a convenient toilet.

Scented with pipe smoke, turpentine, and linseed oil, the main room was kept scrupulously clean, even the wooden floor beneath Rockwell's palette-stand, with its boxes for colors and mixing medium and its white milk glass surface. Extra easels in other parts of the room might hold color sketches in progress, or perhaps a print of a Rembrandt or a Picasso that especially interested Rockwell. Half the time, Rockwell sat in a wooden, armless Windsor chair as he painted, resting his hand on the painting stick placed across the canvas. When he stood, it was sometimes with one foot resting on the base of the easel.

The models who came to the studio were treated like honored guests, whether they were adults or children. Rockwell had worked in Hollywood with some of the day's most famous actors, but he was down-to-earth and genuine when it came to his relationships with ordinary people: one Arlington resident remembered that even when he said a casual hello on the street, he treated others as if they were important to him.

Rose Hoyt, who was several months pregnant with her ninth child at the time, posed for both *Freedom of Speech* and *Freedom of Worship*. Before she sat for *Worship*, Rockwell made a point to ask Mrs. Hoyt whether she minded being portrayed with rosary beads, as a Catholic, which she was not. She considered it thoughtful of him to ask. Posing for three photographic sessions, Mrs. Hoyt earned $15, which in wartime could be put to very good use for her family.

With the photographer snapping the shutter at his direction, Rockwell in a flannel shirt and khaki pants or blue jeans would nimbly move around the models, showing them expressions and positions. He always thoroughly explained to them the story behind the painting and their characters. Over the years he had served as a model, himself, sometimes dressing up in costume, making faces and taking pratfalls for the camera.

Rockwell was also considered a good amateur actor by his friends, and once even took a leading role with Elizabeth Schaeffer in a play put on by a community theater group. He was far less sure of himself when it came to painting the *Four Freedoms*, saying he got a bad case of stage fright at the outset and was unable to make any real progress for more than two months.

He wrote: "It was a job that should have been tackled by Michelangelo."

The *Four Freedoms* were more serious subjects than the usual Rockwell painting, and part of his difficulty with the second painting, *Freedom of Worship*, was that his initial concept for it was not serious enough to him.

"Most of the trouble stemmed from the fact that religion is an extremely delicate subject," he said. "It is so easy to hurt so many people's feelings."

He had worked up that cheery scene in a country barbershop, with recognizable "types" sitting around chatting pleasantly: a Jewish man in the chair, waiting for a shave by a white Protestant barber, while a congenial Catholic priest and slender Anglo-Saxon sat with an elderly black man. Rockwell wanted to emphasize the idea of religious and social harmony, "all of them laughing and getting on well together."

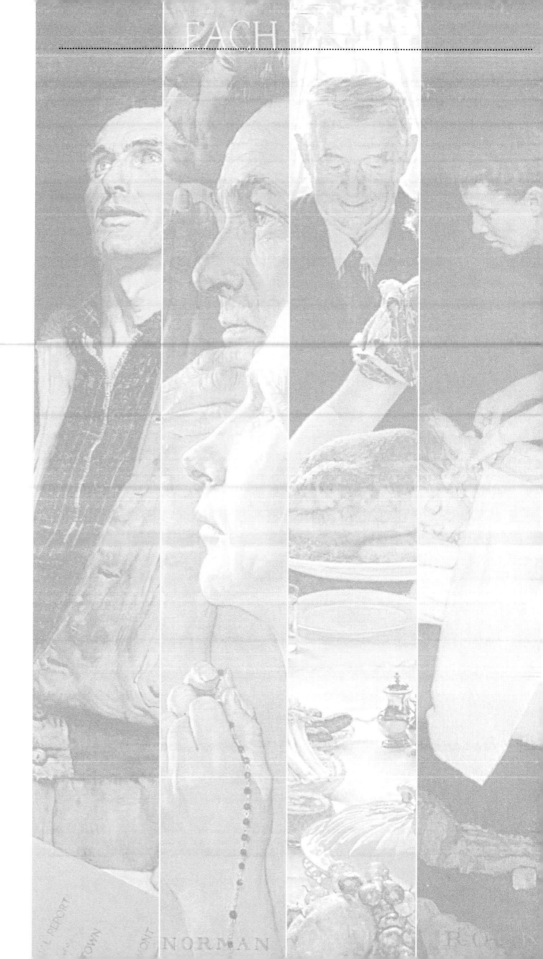

Color Plates

Freedom of Speech
1943

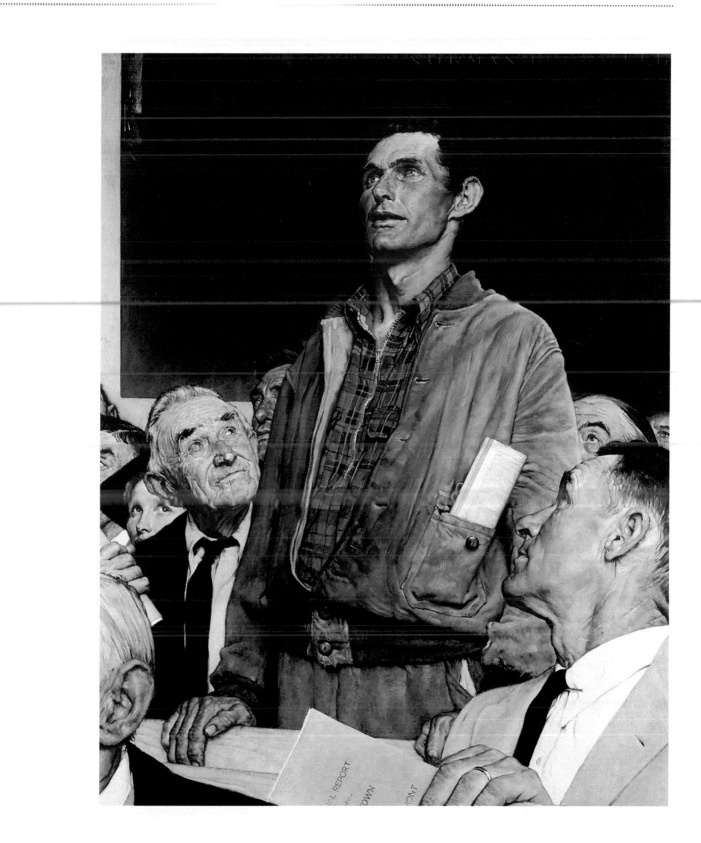

Freedom of Worship
1943

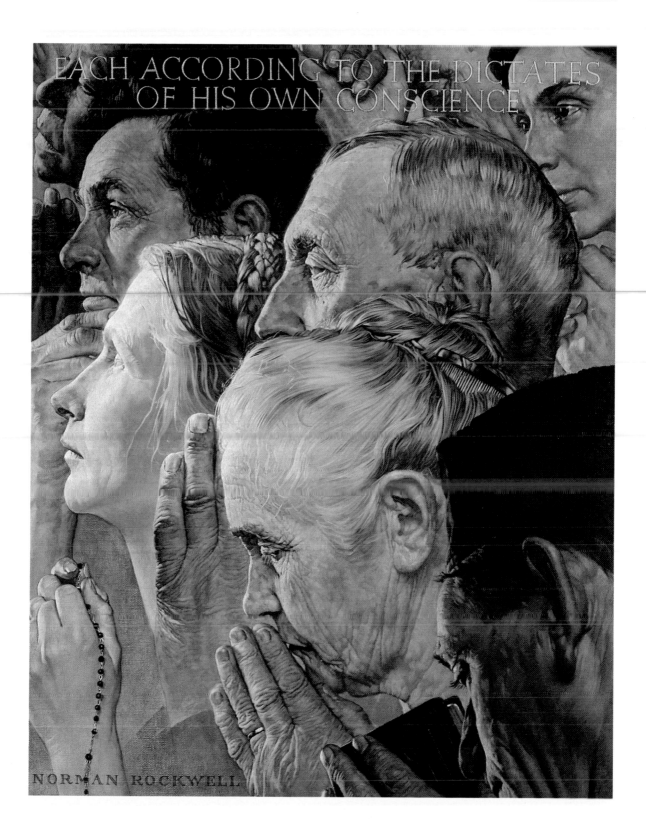

Freedom from Want
1943

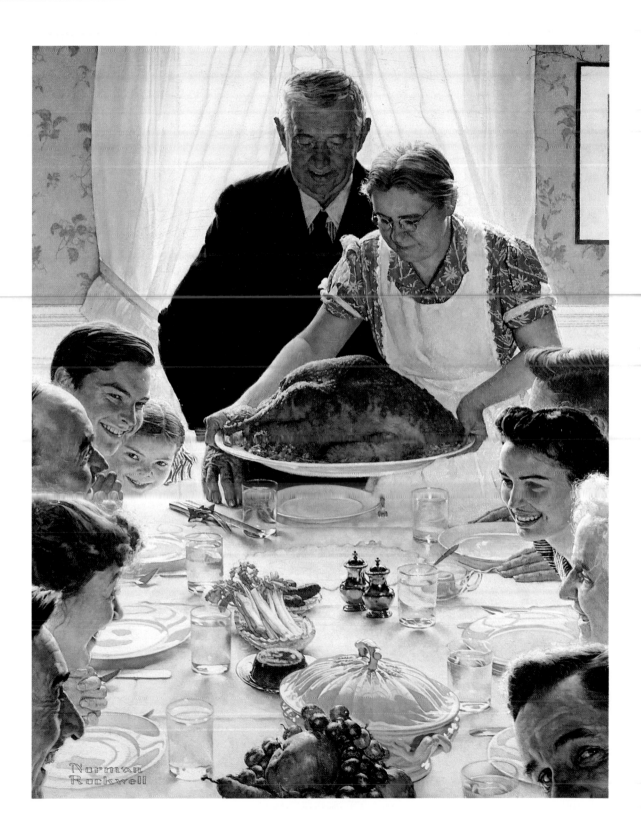

Norman
Rockwell

Freedom from Fear
1943

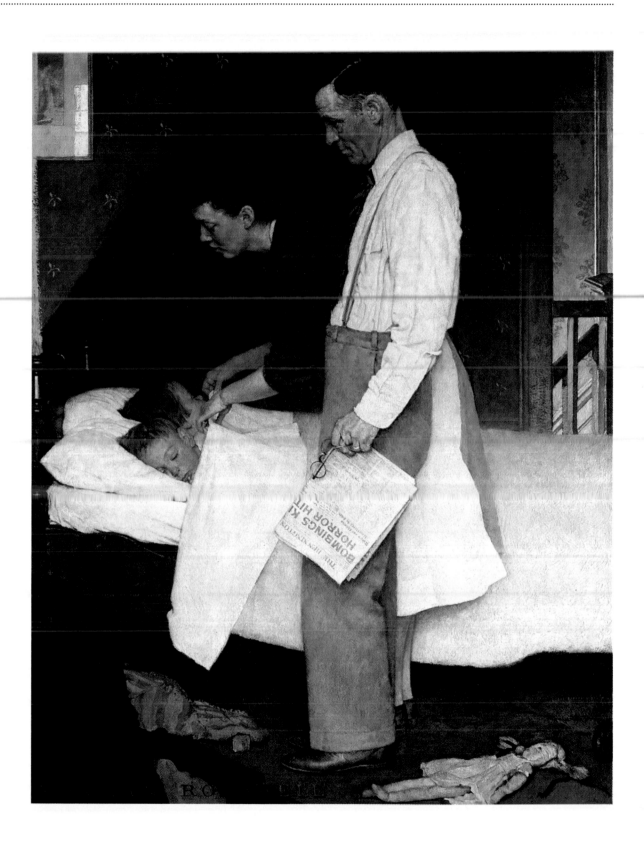

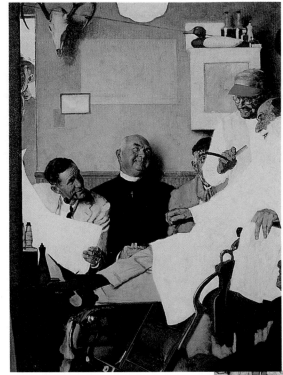

Freedom of Worship
(Preliminary Idea)
1942

Rockwell often set scenes in a barbershop, a typical community gathering place. By depicting people of different religions and backgrounds conversing pleasantly together, he was representing American acceptance of religious diversity. Ultimately, deciding the scene was too difficult to understand as a portrayal of freedom of worship, he rejected it in favor of the composition grouping faces and hands in prayerful and contemplative poses.

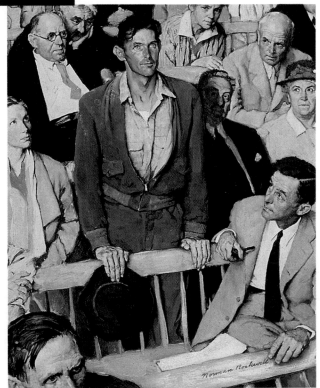

Freedom of Speech
(Study)
1942

One of several attempts at Freedom of Speech, this version lacked focus, Rockwell felt; the viewer saw too broad a scene in the meeting hall, rather than concentrating on the speaker, as in the final painting.

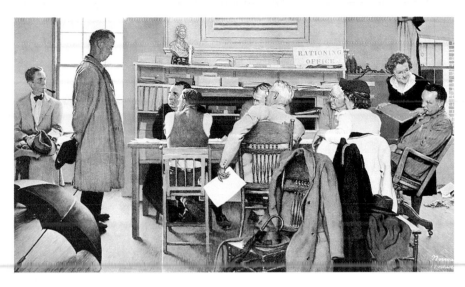

Norman Rockwell Visits a Ration Board

1944

The "Norman Rockwell Visits" series of Illustrations in the *Saturday Evening Post* captured daily life at the home front during World War II. Pictured here is a local committee that decided on individual cases related to wartime limits on consumption of such commodities as food and gasoline. The series also continued after the war.

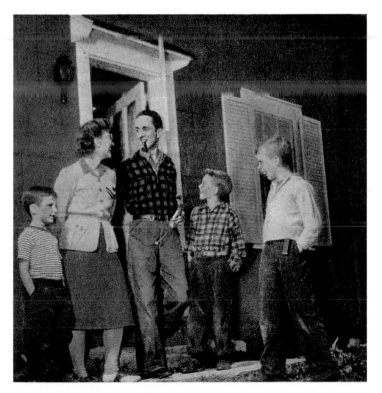

The Rockwell Family

The *Saturday Evening Post* featured this photo of Rockwell and his family at their Vermont home in an article introducing the Four Freedoms series. The celebration of the "common man," a theme central to the Four Freedoms paintings, is also expressed by this scene of the Rockwells as an ordinary American family.

War News

1944

Originally intended as a *Post* cover but never used for that purpose, this painting nevertheless became, over the years, one of Rockwell's best known wartime works. Set in a restaurant in Manchester, Vermont, the scene portrays the intense concentration on a war news broadcast, as the characters pause to listen carefully.

Rosie the Riveter

1943

Industrial work by women was critical to war production during World War II. Rockwell honored that contribution with this image of Rosie the Riveter. He copied the pose from Michelangelo's depiction of the prophet Isaiah on the Sistine Chapel ceiling, and added a halo above her visor. There was no mistaking what this effort was for: she rests her foot on a copy of Adolph Hitler's *Mein Kampf*.

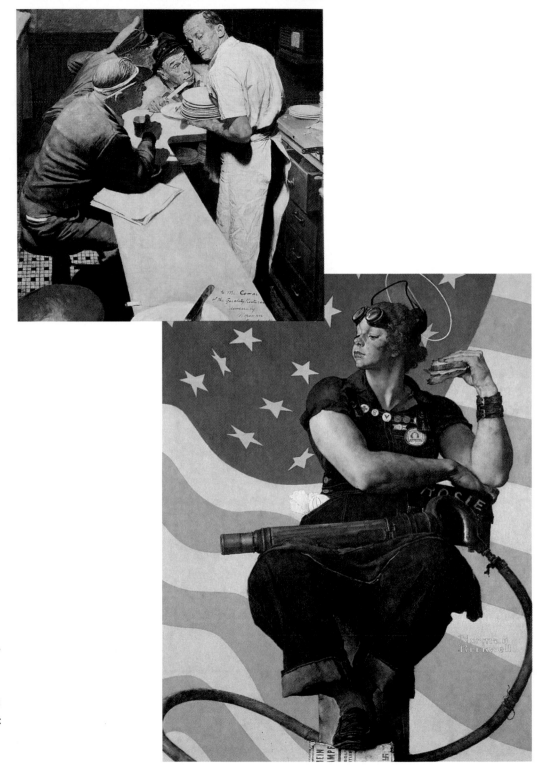

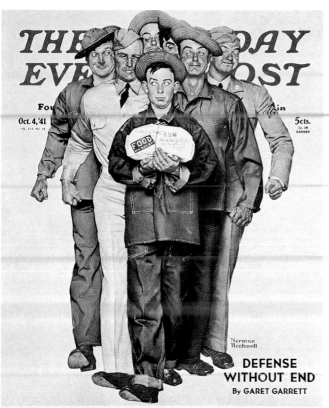

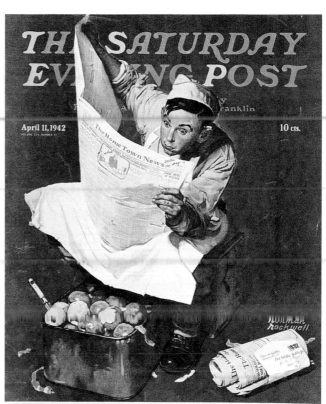

Willie Gillis covers: Food Package and Home Town News

1941 and 1942

Perhaps the best known soldier who never existed, Rockwell's Willie Gillis found his way onto eleven *Post* covers during the war. Willie appeared as a raw and uncertain recruit in 1941, matured through the war, and became a veteran in college in 1946.

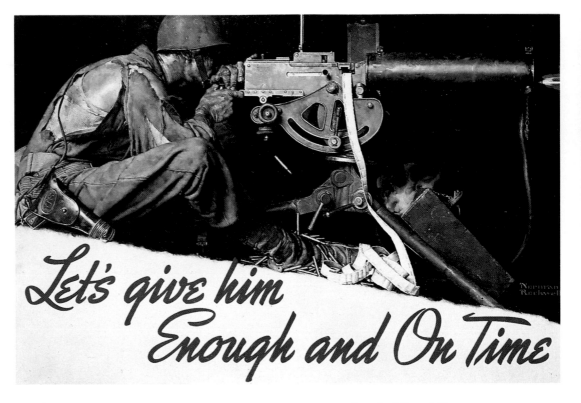

Let's Give Him Enough and On Time

1942

Rockwell painted his first World War II poster for the U.S. Army Ordnance Department. Arranged through the Artists' Guild, the poster was part of the "Keep 'Em Shooting" program, which called for increased production in weapons plants.

Mine America's Coal

1944

Rockwell's portrayal of an American coal miner, wearing two stars for family members in the service, was used by the Office of Emergency Management's War Manpower Commission to encourage employment in war-related industries.

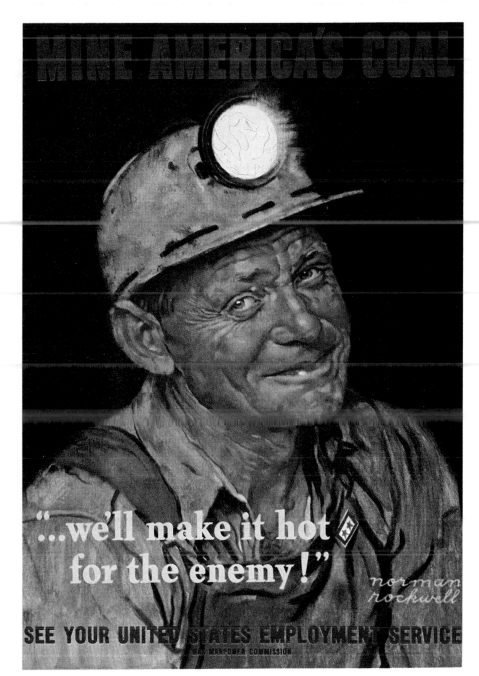

MINE AMERICA'S COAL

"...we'll make it hot for the enemy!"

norman rockwell

SEE YOUR UNITED STATES EMPLOYMENT SERVICE

WAR MANPOWER COMMISSION

Hasten the Homecoming

1945

This scene published at the end of the war used a neighborhood in the back streets of Troy, New York, as a setting. First a *Post* cover, the painting was also used by the War Finance Division of the Treasury as a poster for the final War Loan drive, the Victory Loan.

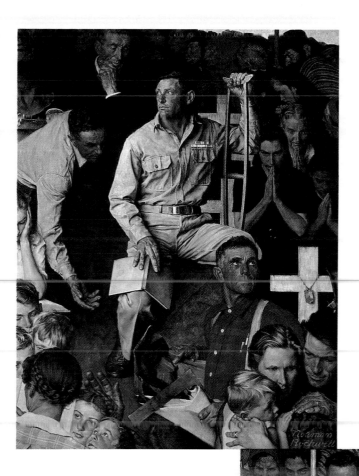

The Long Shadow of Lincoln

1945

Created near the end of the war to illustrate a Carl Sandburg story of this title, the painting shows a group of people of diverse races and backgrounds, free from oppression, free to worship and express themselves, and provided with education to create a decent life. In the center, the disabled veteran and the cross with the dog tag symbolize the sacrifices made for the war.

The Golden Rule

1961

An appeal for cultural, racial, and religious tolerance, The Golden Rule was based on an earlier depiction of the United Nations; Rockwell viewed the U.N. as the best hope for peace in the world. Rockwell never completed the large-scale United Nations painting, but used part of that original concept for The Golden Rule. A mosaic of the painting is now at the United Nations headquarters in New York.

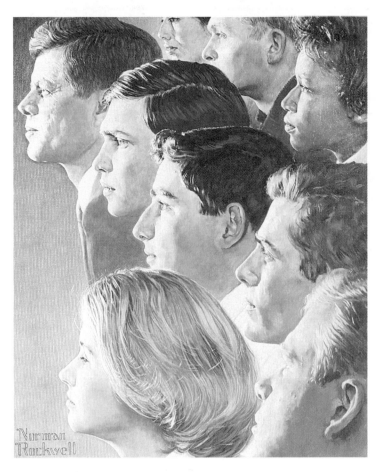

Peace Corps: JFK's Bold Legacy

The Problem We All Live With

1966 and 1964

Rockwell continued to express his ideas about world issues and American responsibilities throughout the rest of his career, as in these contrasting images created for *Look* magazine: school integration in New Orleans, and Peace Corps volunteers, which echoes the style of Freedom of Worship. Rockwell affirmed his commitment to his work's message in these words from a 1963 lecture: "Now I am wildly excited about painting contemporary subjects... pictures about civil rights, astronauts, Peace Corps, the poverty program."

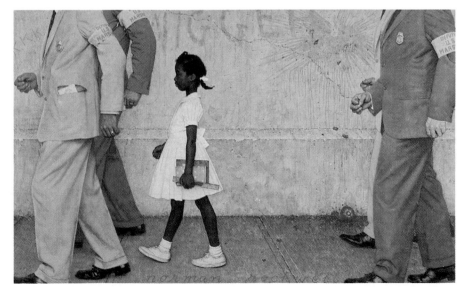

Just when he was almost finished with the painting, however, he decided to start all over. "It was no good," he said. "The situation bordered on the ridiculous." Moreover, when visitors were asked their opinions, few liked his depictions of all the characters. Blacks and Jews did not like his portrayals, and the Catholics said, "Priests don't look like that."

Rockwell started over, but his next idea did not succeed either. He started a third time, and discarded that, too. He was feeling the strain, becoming cross with the children, impatient when they came into the studio to show him turtles or frogs they had caught. By October, when the art editor of the *Post* came up to ask where the *Four Freedoms* were, Rockwell uncharacteristically "snarled politely" that he was working as fast as he could.

What little relaxation Rockwell took in those months usually came in the form of occasional cocktail hours with the Schaeffers before dinner, or badminton on a court set up in the barn. Sometimes there were hikes with the family and friends up to Rattlesnake Rock on Red Mountain behind the house, with their German shepherd dog, Raleigh, in the lead. They made their way through old apple orchards and along forgotten stone walls, into the birch, pine, and oak forest that was rapidly taking on the blush of autumn.

The leaves changed, withered, and the air grew cold, but Rockwell had not yet found the final idea for *Freedom of Worship*, though it was only the second painting of four. He had put himself under great pressure, and no one but he could do anything about it.

The war news, at least, seemed to be improving. American troops had gone on the offensive in the Pacific, landing on Guadalcanal, and it was reported that the German advance in southern Russia had been halted at Stalingrad, where the defenders were fighting house-to-house in the rubble of their city. Now, however, there was strict food and gasoline rationing at home, and in North Africa the brilliant German "Desert Fox," Field Marshal Erwin Rommel, was still threatening the vital Suez Canal.

With headline news of military developments constantly reminding him of the profound meaning behind the freedoms, and with gentle but firm pressure from the *Post*, Rockwell tried again and again to paint *Freedom of Worship*. When at last he broke through, he later recalled, it was as if he had "wrenched the sketch of the final version . . . out of my head and painted it."

This work is a departure from Rockwell's established, story-telling style. The painting shows a close grouping of profiles in prayerful contemplation, lit by a soft, almost golden light. The people vary in age, race, and religion, and above them is the phrase, "Each according to the dictates of his own conscience."

Rockwell had come up with the phrase, but had no idea of its source. He asked Mary, friends, and even the models to try to find out. When interviewed years later, Rose Hoyt recalled that "he had everybody looking through books to see if there was any reason he couldn't use it, whether there was a copyright on it." (It was not until after the publication of *Worship* that letter-writers told him the phrase was similar to one in a text written by nineteenth-century Mormon leader Joseph Smith in his "Principles of Worship.")

In late November, *Freedom from Want* went along pretty much as planned, some of the photographs being taken at the family's Thanksgiving dinner, when Rockwell's mother came to visit and was included in the painting. The family cook, Mrs. Thaddeus Wheaton, was photographed placing the holiday turkey on the table that extends below the edge of the canvas, as if inviting the viewer to join in the feast.

That Rockwell was grappling with weariness by this time is recalled by Shirley Hoisington, who had posed in the studio as the little girl at the far end of the table. Though only six at the time, she sensed that Rockwell was short-tempered as he gave instructions and Pelham took photographs. By now, Rockwell had lost ten pounds from his already thin frame, but did not allow himself to stop.

At last, in mid-winter, Rockwell finished *Freedom from Fear*, portraying a young mother tucking in her two sleeping children, while the pensive father stands nearby, holding a newspaper with headlines about foreign cities being bombed. Rockwell meant it to say, "Thank God we can put our children to bed at night with a feeling of security, knowing they will not be killed in the night."

This painting had held close to its original concept as Rockwell had first thought of it during the 1940 air war known as "The Battle of Britain," according to Dorothy Lawrence, the model for the mother. Mrs. Lawrence posed twice for this subject in that year, and moved away from Arlington in the summer of 1942, before the final version was painted as *Freedom from Fear*. Rockwell asked the local newspaper, the *Bennington Banner*, to mock up a dummy edition with the headline about bombing as a prop.

By comparison with the difficulties in creating *Freedom of Speech* and *Freedom of Worship*, Rockwell had very little trouble with the last two paintings. Yet his portrayal of these two freedoms did not please him, as he wrote in his autobiography: "I never liked 'Freedom from Fear' or, for that matter, 'Freedom from Want.' Neither of them has any wallop."

More than the paintings' lack of "wallop" bothered him, however. It was a time when occupied Europe was suffering food shortages, and Rockwell thought *Freedom from Want* seemed to represent "overabundance, the table was so loaded down with food." As for *Freedom from Fear*, he thought he had based it "on a rather smug idea," when London was being bombed night after night.

"I think the two I had the most trouble with — 'Freedom of Speech' and 'Freedom of Worship' — have more of an impact, say more, better." He considered *Freedom of Worship* the best of all.

The four paintings were framed and briefly put on display at the West Arlington Grange before being crated and shipped off to the *Post* in Philadelphia. It was the end of January, 1943, and Rockwell was utterly exhausted after an unprecedented seven months of the most difficult work he had ever undertaken. He said the *Four Freedoms* were "serious paintings which sucked the energy right out of me like dredges, leaving me dazed and thoroughly weary."

Within days, Rockwell was back at the easel, painting his first "April Fool" cover for the Post, not as work, but as "the perfect relaxation." It showed an old man and woman in their living room, happily playing checkers without checkers, wearing ice skates and roller skates and surrounded by craziness, such as a deer dozing under a chair, pictures on the wall that were alive, and fish leaping a cascade that rushed down the steps.

By comparison with the large *Four Freedoms*, which were almost three feet by four feet, the April Fool cover was "tiny . . . the exact size of the *Post* — and nuts. I didn't have to worry about mistakes or authenticity or saying something."

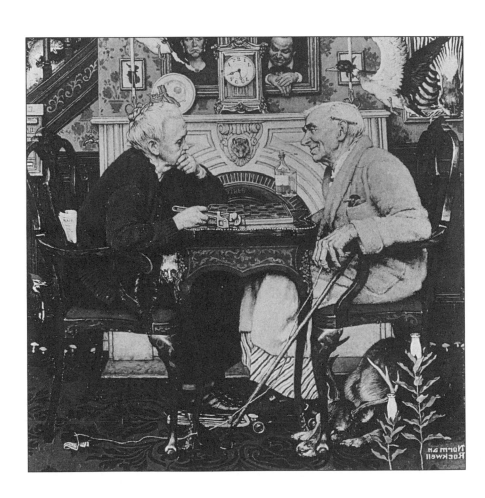

After months of difficult work on his *Four Freedoms* paintings, Rockwell relaxed with this April Fool scene, the first of a series that appeared on *Post* covers.

Part Three

The Nation's Four Freedoms

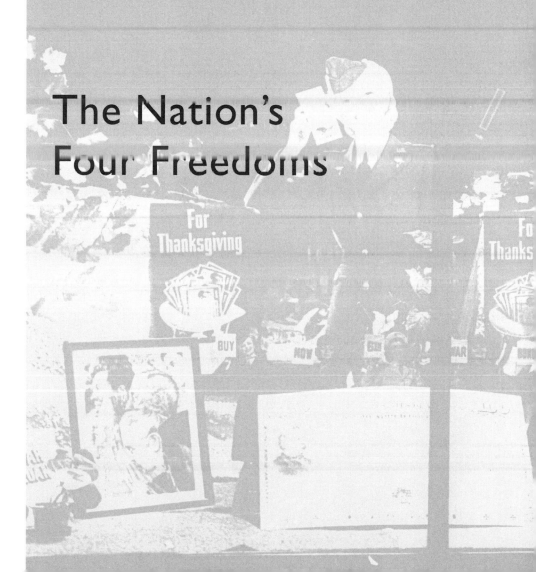

A store window in
St. Louis: Rockwell's
Four Freedoms images
were prominent in
homes, businesses, and
workplaces throughout
the country.

By January, 1943, World War II had taken a painful toll on the United States, with more than 20,000 American dead and scores of thousands severely wounded. This sacrifice, however, had helped achieve substantial military progress against the Axis.

The Allied landings in North Africa and the subsequent campaign had been a success, with Rommel's forces backed against the wall in Tunisia. At the same time in Stalingrad, the Russians had surrounded a huge but hungry German army that was suffering slow death from the dual onslaught of the merciless Russian winter and vengeful Russian troops who had been resupplied with American weaponry.

The tide of war had not yet turned, but Roosevelt's outlook at the opening of 1943 was far better than in 1940-41, when he had written his original Four Freedoms speech. "The New Year's Eve in the White House was a much more cheerful affair than it had been in 1941," recalled Samuel Rosenman, a speech writer for the president.

The president and Mrs. Roosevelt and their guests drank hearty champagne toasts to the United States and to the United Nations. Then, at his wife's suggestion and along with millions of others around the world, Roosevelt offered a moving toast to family and friends who were unable to be at home that night.

Roosevelt was to give his annual address to Congress in a few days. Despite all his country's trials, there was much to be proud of, including the success of the great war-production machine he had helped put in motion. Back in 1941, he had been fiercely criticized by political opponents for setting national production goals that had been termed "fantastic" and "demagogic." By 1943, however, those goals had been reached and surpassed.

Where in the autumn of 1942 there had been only three aircraft carriers in the American fleet, there soon would be fifty in active service. New American-made tanks by the thousands were racing across the North African desert, or taking up Russian defensive positions in the frozen tundra. Millions of tons of American bombs were steadily dropping from Allied planes flying over Germany and Japan. This astounding and ever-growing triumph of military production was the focus of Roosevelt's speech to the combined houses of Congress.

He said, "These facts and figures . . . will give no great aid and comfort to the enemy. . . . I suspect that Hitler and Tojo will find it difficult to explain to the German and Japanese people just why it is that 'decadent, inefficient democracy' can produce such phenomenal quantities of weapons and munitions — and fighting men."

Yet, there was a long way to go before the war would be won, because Roosevelt and Churchill were determined that it be fought without relent until the Axis powers surrendered — unconditionally. At the end of January, 1943, these two leaders appeared at Casablanca, Morocco, and publicly announced this grim resolve.

Unconditional surrender, their statement said, "does not mean the destruction of the population of Germany, Italy, and Japan, but it does mean the destruction of the philosophies in those countries which are based on conquest and the subjugation of other people."

Demanding the enemy's unconditional surrender, Americans well knew, meant that despite the success of the country's military and industrial effort, more years of war and destruction lay ahead. No one knew when or how it would end. With an entire generation of young people mobilized to fight, there was little comfort to be found in the improving war news.

Historian James MacGregor Burns described this difficult, grinding period in the middle of World War II as it affected ordinary Americans: "The wartime restrictions on almost everyone's individual liberty, the continued subordination of women and blacks, the contrast between the material well-being of millions of Americans and the ceaseless sorrow of those who had lost fathers, brothers, and sons (and the first few mothers, sisters, and daughters) . . . should have sharpened questions about the fundamental meaning of the war.

"Yes, avenging Pearl Harbor — yes, beating Hitler — yes, winning, winning, winning — but beyond that, what? . . . The vast majority had no notion — or only the foggiest — of the Atlantic Charter or of the freedoms the nation was defending."

Norman Rockwell's four new paintings would bring into clear focus those freedoms for which Americans were fighting, and would do so at one of the bleaker hours of the war.

When *Saturday Evening Post* editor Ben Hibbs received Norman Rockwell's *Four Freedoms* paintings that January, he was both moved and thrilled. To him they were an "inspiration . . . in the same way that the clock tower of old Independence Hall, which I can see from my office window, inspires me.

"If this be Fourth of July talk, so be it. Maybe this country needs a bit more Fourth of July the year round."

Regarding *Speech* and *Worship*, Hibbs said that even though art critics might consider them no more than examples of the best in illustration, he disagreed. "To me they are great human documents in the form of paint and canvas. A great picture, I think, is one which moves and inspires millions of people. The *Four Freedoms* did — and do."

On February 13 the *Post* published "Cover Man," a long article by Jack Alexander about the career of Rockwell. The article opened by saying, "Norman Rockwell, whose series of paintings on the Four Freedoms will begin in the *Post* next week, discovered the Century of the Common Man a generation before the statesmen did. This was appropriate enough, for great painters — and great novelists, poets and essayists — have always jumped the gun on history while the political leaders were squatting back on their haunches awaiting an audible signal or a significantly planted boot."

Alexander went on to describe Rockwell's work: "Year after year he has gone on portraying the Common Man . . . and the Common Man's wife, his children, his pastor, his doctor, his garage mechanic, his druggist, his grocer, his barber, his flivver, his dog and his neighbors.

"Rockwell's Common Man was earthily American. He raised no clenched fist and carried no banner demanding anything, and he didn't incite anyone to riot. . . . [He] asked only his rights as an American and silently pledged his faith in the promise of his country and in the system under which he lived and raised his family."

Many Americans were willing to believe that Rockwell was just like the familiar characters seen in his paintings. Of course, he was more complex and far more ambitious than the one-dimensional "Common Man" described by Alexander. Yet, Rockwell was stamped for life by this description, and so was his work. Though intended as a compliment, the *Post*'s effusive and oversimple characterization of the illustrator served the public-relations purposes of the magazine far more than it illuminated the true character of Norman Rockwell. Still, he did not publicly complain, for it was all part of the life of a famous "cover man."

Before the *Post* ran Rockwell's freedoms paintings in four consecutive weekly issues beginning on February 20, President Roosevelt was solicited by the magazine to write a letter praising them. Roosevelt first saw reproductions of the freedoms early that month, and his letter of commendation to the *Post* is dated February 10.

This letter, addressed to associate editor Forrest Davis, is similar to one Roosevelt wrote for Rockwell at the same time. In fact, the White House gave the *Post* a draft of the president's letter to Rockwell and left it up to the magazine to make revisions and produce an "official" letter to thank the *Post* for publishing the Four Freedoms. Roosevelt's personal letter to Rockwell is friendly, while the official letter to the *Post* is formal and also mentions the four related essays that were to be published with the paintings.

In the Rockwell letter, Roosevelt wrote, "I think you have done a superb job in bringing home to the plain, everyday citizen the plain, everyday truths behind the Four Freedoms. . . . I congratulate you not alone on the execution but also for the spirit which impelled you to make this contribution to the common cause of a freer, happier world.

"They tell me that you made use of your neighbors at Arlington, Vermont, as models for the intensely human and very American people in the paintings. The roots of democracy run deep in Vermont and, in drawing upon the life about you, you have tapped those roots."

The Roosevelt letter to the *Post* says, "This is the first pictorial representation I have seen of the staunchly American values contained in the rights of free speech and free worship and our goals of freedom from fear and want."

Remarking on the essays, the letter states, "Their words should inspire all who read them with a deeper appreciation of the way of life we are striving to preserve."

Roosevelt wanted the essays translated into foreign languages and presented, along with reproductions of the paintings, to leaders of the United Nations. The White House suggested that the *Post* go to the Office of War Information to arrange for the translations. This was all in keeping with Roosevelt's intent to use the four freedoms as international symbols of democracy.

Starting on February 20, the *Post* ran one Rockwell painting in each successive issue, following the sequence in which the freedoms were laid out in Roosevelt's original speech. They were published inside in full-color, full-page presentations, each opposite the essay with the same title.

For the essays on the four freedoms, Ben Hibbs had his pick of the top writers in the country, many of whom were regular contributors to the *Post*. His choice for the first, "Freedom of Speech," was the widely admired dean of popular American letters, Booth Tarkington, a Pulitzer Prize-winning novelist and a dramatist.

A week later, on February 27, *Freedom of Worship* ran, along with an essay by best-selling writer and lecturer on history and philosophy, Will Durant. In his mid-fifties, Durant was at the height of his fame, and busy with his ten-volume life's work, *The Story of Civilization*.

On March 6, *Freedom from Want* was published alongside an essay by Carlos Bulosan. An unknown, impoverished Filipino poet in his twenties, Bulosan was struggling to survive in the United States; he had emigrated at sixteen. *Post* editors who had seen his work thought Bulosan would be the appropriate choice for writing about "Freedom from Want" because he had never yet experienced that freedom. Though he was an itinerant worker wandering somewhere on the West Coast, the magazine managed to track him down and offered him the golden chance to write the article.

Former OWI staffer Stephen Vincent Benét, famous as a poet, novelist, and short-story writer, wrote "Freedom from Fear." Benét was forty-four when he wrote the essay, one of his last literary works, for he died on March 13, 1943, the very day it was published by the *Post*.

From the first, the *Four Freedoms* paintings were a nationwide triumph. Letters of praise inundated the *Post*'s head office, requests for copies poured in, and editor Ben Hibbs took pride in the immediate effect Rockwell's paintings had on war-weary America.

"The result astonished us all," Hibbs said. "These four pictures quickly became the best known and most appreciated paintings of that era. The . . . American people needed the inspirational message which they conveyed so forcefully and so beautifully."

The response was unprecedented. More than 25,000 readers promptly ordered sets of full-color reproductions suitable for framing. The offer in the *Post* anticipated the "widespread public demand," and with a touch of salesmanship, the announcement added that "because of the paper shortage, the number must be limited."

The accompanying essay was printed on the same sheet with the reproduction of the painting so that both could be framed as one piece. The cost of a full set of four was twenty-five cents, "in stamps or coin," which the magazine said was no more than the cost of printing. Along with each set of reproductions and essays was a copy of Jack Alexander's life story of Rockwell.

By recognizing Rockwell's gift for expressing what was foremost on the minds of the American public, Hibbs had pulled off a brilliant and unparalleled success for his struggling magazine. Americans might be vague on the politics of the war, but they clearly understood and appreciated Rockwell's *Four Freedoms*, and they wrote about it to him — in more than 60,000 letters.

Here is a sampling of what they said:

For your noble and human and deeply stirring series interpreting The Four Freedoms, I want to send my warmest appreciation and admiration. I feel the more personally grateful because three members of my family are in service, one in New Guinea. Your great pictures will help much to keep America's head high and its purposes true.

Carlton C. Wells
Ann Arbor, Michigan

In the past six years, my husband has been working day and night to fulfill his promise to help the working man and give him a voice in this great land of ours.

He brought your picture ("Speech") home and said, "Now look and study it. Everything I have done in the past and all that I hope to accomplish in the future is shown in this picture."

Every town hall in the land should have one on its walls

Mrs. John A. Flannery
Pittsburgh

Of course I realize you are tired to death of receiving letters from people who "like" your work. However, I cannot refrain from telling you how much I appreciate the first in your series of paintings. . . . "Freedom of Speech" recalls so many of the little town meetings I have attended as a young chap in Vermont and later as a newspaperman, and brings back to me some of the independence of thought and freedom of spirit which was always the essence of these meetings.

E.J. Lyndes, Editor
The Rochester Courier
Rochester, New Hampshire

I've come downstairs, Mr. Rockwell, in a middle of the night moment of wakefulness, to have another session with your "Freedom of Speech."

My tools, you see, are screwdrivers and pliers and springhooks — not words. But somehow it is born in upon me, I must try to tell you what you have done for us all.

You are exactly right. There is just enough in that canvas for your purpose, but I can feel and see the parts of the room that lie beyond your boundaries — we're all there, the deep sincerity of purpose that blacks out personal inhibitions and timidity; the old chappie is there who speaks out at <u>every</u> gathering, the chap who relishes the taste of five syllable words and the decorative rhetoric; yes, and in another corner is the old lady who is always called upon to express her sentiments, apropos or not, but the feather on her hat, bedraggled with many a sun and rain, bobs giddily and emphatically just the same; and there are the youngsters, too, striving mightily to order their thoughts and praying for whatever it is that gives quiet to the knees and the fluent tongue. Yes, and thank God, the old heads, the level heads in which there is no longer heat or malice or personal ambition. We look again. There can be no doubt. This meeting, this precious gift of Free Speech — we're getting somewhere!

Thank you, Mr. Rockwell, for your reassurance!

Paul L. Brandt
Carlisle, Pennsylvania

I am European born and have lived and worked as fashion editor and designer in the big cities of Europe, and have come over to California 8 years ago from Paris, <u>not</u> <u>as</u> <u>a</u> <u>refugee</u>, but because I've always admired America and its creed. I consider you as the man, who has, up till now, brought the American people visually near to me. . . . By now, I've cut out the first of your paintings and am going to keep it.

Lily Nagy
Hollywood, California

You paid much attention to detail in drawing that wrinkled gray jacket (in "Speech"). Being a New Englander myself, I can appreciate that touch. It represents to me a part of America, as definite a part as the town meeting. Nowhere is there a type of government as democratic as the town meeting, where all rules, laws and restrictions can be argued and thrashed out by those who will be immediately affected by them.

I am indeed thankful that I am able to help defend that right.

Richard Morrison
U.S. Army Air Corps Maxwell Field, Alabama

Although words are our business, this is one time when they are very feeble indeed.

It remained for you to capture the real spirit of "The Four Freedoms" as it lives in the hearts of the plain people of America. Yours is easily the most moving appeal of all the appeals directed at the winning of the war, and I am very proud to know the man whose brush was responsible for it.

Joseph Katz
The Joseph Katz Company, Advertising
Hollywood, California

A letter to Rockwell written by a member of Congress from Massachusetts included a copy of her proposed resolution to recognize officially a fifth freedom, "Freedom of Private Enterprise."

It would be very fine if you could contribute a drawing to further public interest in this worthy objective. . . . If it is possible to incorporate this idea in the cover you are planning to do for a future issue of the Saturday Evening Post, it undoubtedly would be a major contribution towards speedy passage of the Resolution.

Edith Nourse Rogers
Washington, D.C.

Roderick Stephens, chairman of the Bronx Inter-Racial Conference, was so impressed by Rockwell's execution of the freedoms that he asked the artist to paint something equally as strong that would promote interracial relations. It was a time of ferocious race riots in a number of cities, including Los Angeles, Houston, and Detroit — a time, said Stephens, when blacks, who were largely not blessed with freedom from want, were at that moment also denied freedom from fear.

Stephens offered to work with Rockwell to conceptualize an appropriate subject. He suggested that a series of posters might be developed which would illustrate how blacks have contributed to the common good and have helped America in specific ways to realize the four freedoms so revered by President Roosevelt. It would be a series complementary to the "Four Freedoms" series, said Stephens.

> To this conclusion . . . I believe you, individually, can make a contribution of more significance perhaps than any other individual.
>
> I am attempting to suggest an idea which . . . can be visualized by you, in terms to which the American public will quickly respond. If so, you can thus advance racial goodwill by years, and . . . you will be making a contribution of unmeasurable significance to the nation of today and the world of tomorrow.
>
> Roderick Stephens
> New York, NY
> Chairman,
> Bronx Inter-Racial Conference

(Rockwell corresponded with Stephens, and in subsequent work addressed directly and eloquently the subject of race relations a number of times, although not in any specific series of paintings.)

Not all the letters about the *Four Freedoms* paintings were favorable, and there was plenty of criticism and advice in some others:

Please Sir accept my sincerest compliment for your most marvelous picturization of "FREEDOM OF WORSHIP." . . . But, Mr. Rockwell . . . is there not enough character in the faces of YOUTH for an artist to portray and use in a subject like this. . . . After all these kindly dear and revered people that you portray are sweet, lovely and picturesque.

But their lives are about at an end, and they in the majority have Christ and Religion closely at heart. But youth is trying desperately to find itself, and what better way can it than through Christ, Prayer and Worship of God?

Theodore R. Bohn
Chicago

The FOUR FREEDOMS guaranteed to Americans by the "Bill of Rights" . . . are Freedom of Religion, Freedom of Speech, Freedom of the Press, Freedom of Assembly.

When President Roosevelt or Vice-president Wallace speak of "the 4 freedoms" they are talking about something of their own invention, for they have eliminated the third and fourth, and put in their place those utopian promises so popular with all dictators, freedom from fear and freedom from want. . . .

By freedom from want and freedom from fear they mean that if the people will give up their independence and do what the government tells them, the government will take care of them. . . .

Why don't you make pictures of the American Freedoms instead of the New Deal Freedoms? I greatly admire the first two you have done.

T.R. Grant
New York City

I want to tell you very strongly of how very bad I think your picture of "Freedom of Worship" is.

Here are my criticisms. Although I know nothing about your art, I do know something about life, having lived.

1. In your picture there are six principal faces in view — now five are old and one is at least thirtyish. Where are the youths and the children, who are certainly of greater importance than the old?

2. All are foreign-looking — where is the "Yankee"?

3. All look northeast Nordic or Jew — where is the old American type and the negro and the Italian type?

4. All are laborers and poor and worn — where is the middle class and the intellectual, etc.?

5. All are praying with eyes open. Don't many people pray with eyes shut. I know I do. Some must.

6. All are facing the same direction like cattle or sheep, but the distinction of human beings in a free country is that they face opposite directions even toward different gods.

7. All are portrayed in the same dull grey-brown color, where religion should be bright and gay and uplifting (for don't people often go to church arrayed in their gay Easter finery?)

8. The caption "Each according to the dictates of his own conscience" is ill-chosen, because in the viewpoint of many people the Catholics do not worship according to their own conscience but according to the dictates of the Holy Roman Catholic Church.

I can't see how you could have gone so completely wrong; so a letter of explanation would help a little.

T.C. Upham
General Director
The Cape Theatre
Cape May, New Jersey

Rockwell simply replied:

I believe that by this time you have heard from Mr. Yates, art editor of the Post.

I am extremely sorry that you found my picture so bad, and can truly say that in it I tried to express what I felt about Freedom of Worship — which I believe is all anybody can do.

One kindred spirit was visual-entertainment impresario Walt Disney, who wrote, "I thought your Four Freedoms were great. I especially loved the Freedom of Worship and the composition and symbolism expressed in it. It appealed to me very much."

And then there was the letter from the Pioneer Suspender Company, pointing out that the father in *Freedom from Fear* was wearing a pair of Pioneer suspenders. He had good reason to be unafraid, the letter said, as long as his pants were being held up by Pioneers.

In the announcement about the availability of *Four Freedoms* reproductions, the *Post* also explained that the Office of War Information was about to print 2,500,000 posters made from the paintings. Furthermore, stated the magazine with understandable pride, "the four Rockwell originals will go on a tour in a special War-Bond-selling campaign jointly sponsored by the United States Treasury Department and the *Post*."

The previous December had seen the conclusion of the government's first national war-bond campaign, called "The Victory Loan Drive," which had started early in 1942. This key project of Roosevelt and Treasury Secretary Henry Morgenthau had aimed for raising $9 billion but had brought in almost $13 billion. It was, said Morgenthau, "the biggest amount of money ever raised by any government in such a short time."

Compared to the $7 billion per month being spent on the military, the money raised by war-bond drives was far from sufficient. As a nationwide grass-roots program, however, the drives had other functions beyond raising money: millions of Americans

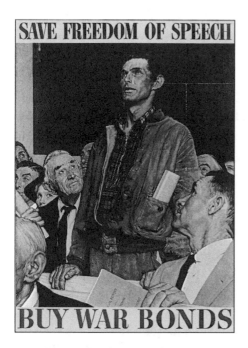

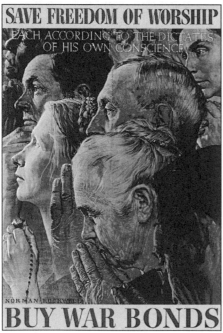

Poster versions of the *Four Freedoms* paintings were created for the Second War Loan Drive.

bought small-denomination series "E" bonds, and Secretary Morgenthau emphasized that it was a tremendous morale booster for people to be able to contribute to the war effort while, at the same time, voluntarily saving. Furthermore, for both Roosevelt and Morgenthau, all the pro-war propaganda attendant to bond drives was extremely crucial.

Rockwell's *Four Freedoms* paintings were the perfect centerpiece of a traveling show created to promote the next war-bond campaign. Called "The Second War Loan Drive," the campaign was designed not only to bring the Treasury desperately needed revenue, but also was a way to "sell the war" to a nation that by now was growing weary of it.

Recent polls indicated that thirty-five per cent of the American people still had no clear idea of why the United States was in the war. An equal number were willing to settle for a separate peace with Germany — this at a time when the firmly declared policy of the United Nations was that no member country would make peace unilaterally with the enemy. Roosevelt had to overcome this national uncertainty, which was a potential obstacle to his policy of prosecuting a total war. War-bond drives were a way for the president to whip up popular support for his war plans because the enormous promotion behind the drives appealed to American patriotism, to the willingness of people to sacrifice for the sake of the fighting men, and to the general hatred of totalitarianism.

Dramatic war-bond posters said "Buy a Share in America," "Bonds for Victory," "Back the Attack," and "Make Your Own Declaration of War." These posters hung in every factory, office, store, and government building. Movie-

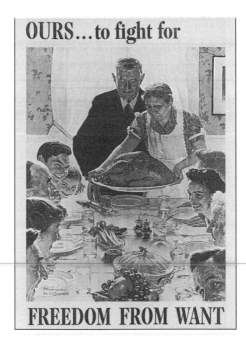

OURS...to fight for

FREEDOM FROM WANT

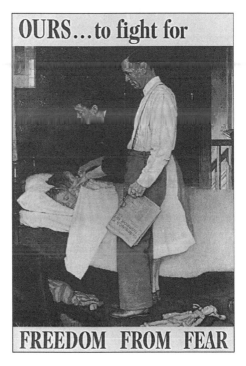

OURS...to fight for

FREEDOM FROM FEAR

theater newsreels, radio broadcasts, feature films, and live stage shows often included appeals to buy small-denomination bonds, which ranged from $25 to $1,000, had a ten-year maturity, and were non-negotiable.

Not only did stars of the entertainment world make free appearances to sell bonds, but most of the publicity, including air-time and advertising space in publications, was provided by the media free of charge. Thus, a great pro-war propaganda machine was financed by the private sector while billions were raised to pay for the war.

Treasury Secretary Morgenthau said the generosity of contributing businesses made it possible to run war-bond drives without "spending one penny on paid advertising in newspapers and magazines or on the radio."

The bond campaign of 1942 had been so successful in both financing the war and per-suading people to support it that a seasoned advertising executive recruited to advise Morgenthau admiringly called him "the number two advertising man in Washington. His only peer is his boss (Roosevelt)."

The 1943 bond drive featuring Rockwell's *Four Freedoms* was expected to be even better. In just a matter of weeks between January and April, 1943, the Treasury and the *Post* organized a massive nationwide itinerary for what was being called the Four Freedoms War Bond Show. With its debut that April at the Hecht Company department store in Washington, D.C., and featuring Rockwell's paintings, the show would inaugurate the new war-bond campaign. Afterwards, it would travel to major retailers around the country and be the main attraction in citywide bond-sales drives.

Anticipating the show's arrival, thousands of volunteers were drummed up in city after city to organize related local events and programs such as public rallies, parades, and personal appearances of film stars and other celebrities to promote war bond sales. The aim of the Four Freedoms Show was to prepare an atmosphere for intense local bond-selling over a short period of time.

The new campaign had developed that winter out of a plan by Roosevelt and the *Post* to stage Four Freedoms ceremonies at defense factories. Radio shows were to accompany these ceremonies, including a promotion on First Lady Eleanor Roosevelt's own "Lands of the Free" broadcast on the Inter-American University of the Air. Once this initial concept became known, businesses, retailers, municipalities, celebrities, politicians, and volunteer organizations were attracted by the appeal of Rockwell's paintings and wanted to be part of it.

Almost overnight, the Four Freedoms Show became the rallying point of a massive national outpouring of patriotic enthusiasm.

The *Post*, with its enormous circulation, was a key to publicizing the Four Freedoms Show and the nationwide war-bonds campaign. Not only was the *Post* supporting the war effort by co-sponsoring the Four Freedoms Show, but the magazine was also earning abundant publicity and goodwill — both much needed at a time when its fortunes were flagging, its future still in doubt.

During the long tenure of editor George Horace Lorimer, the *Post* had been solidly conservative. Lorimer, with his anti-European and anti-internationalist views, had been "crushed and bewildered," according to one biographer, when Roosevelt and his "New Deal" won the election of 1936. Beginning to doubt his own abilities as editor, Lorimer soon retired, but his chosen successor, Wesley Stout, labored to perpetuate the same ultra-conservative views.

Stout virulently opposed Roosevelt's domestic and foreign policies and cast aspersions on liberal social ideas that Lorimer had also objected to as European "isms." Stout described these policies as the work of intellectuals who had no understanding of the real world — certainly not of the realities in the United States. He agreed with Lorimer's terming the New Deal a "discredited European ideology." While no advocate of Fascism, Stout let his isolationist conservatism run away with him once too often when, in the spring of 1942, the *Post* published a right-wing article entitled "The Case Against the Jew."

Stout had sealed his own doom. An enormous public outcry against both the article and magazine was accompanied by cancellations of advertising and subscriptions and even threats of a boycott. Within a month, there was an apology on the editorial page and Ben Hibbs replaced Stout as editor. Hibbs quickly distanced the magazine from Stout's aggressive political conservatism. He changed not only the cover design, but also the focus of the magazine, reducing the amount of fiction and increasing journalistic coverage of the war, which he called "the greatest news story of our time."

Rockwell's *Four Freedoms* paintings came at just the right moment for the *Post*, which wanted to champion the American ideal of self-reliance founded on traditional cornerstones of family and community. With the publishing of Rockwell's *Four Freedoms*, Hibbs established the magazine as a leader in the American war effort. Having the war-bond show identified with the *Saturday Evening Post* positioned the magazine

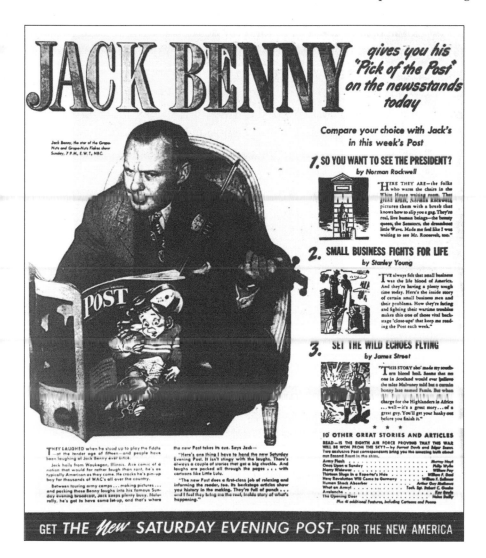

Jack Benny was featured in an advertisement in the *Chicago Tribune* promoting the "new" *Saturday Evening Post;* the ad also highlighted Rockwell's *So You Want To See The President*.

where Hibbs wanted it — firmly in the mainstream of American popular culture.

Early on, the government's Office of War Information took the initiative in the promotional campaign for the bond drive, creating a radio dramatization based on the meaning behind Rockwell's *Four Freedoms*. Broadcast in March by OWI's "Free World Theater," the dramatization was prepared by the Hollywood Writers Mobilization and had an all-star cast. OWI also printed the posters of the four paintings and arranged for their distribution by Boy Scouts to almost 400,000 retailers across the country. OWI soon was receiving more than 2,000 daily requests for posters.

As the 1943 war-bond drive got underway, advertising specialists had been given leadership of OWI, much to the chagrin of the writers' division in OWI's Domestic Branch. The writers believed that OWI's short films and radio spots too often trivialized the real meaning of war and the horrors of combat. They also objected to Hollywood's many feature movies with "hoked-up" war themes that might be strong at the box office but romanticized war and were riddled with stereotypes.

In 1943, three out of ten films made in Hollywood were about the war. Each week, an estimated 85,000,000 Americans sat in movie theaters and soaked up Hollywood's exaggerated depictions of sinister German spies and vicious Japanese fanatics who relished killing innocent civilians. The villains were, of course, always outwitted by American heroes, and at times by cartoon characters. Weekly serials featured such anti-Fascist fighters as Batman, Spiderman, Masked Marvel, Secret Agent X-9, and Spy Smasher. To stay timely, even two-gun cowboy Tom Mix fought it out with a giant fright-balloon called "King Kong," which had been launched in the United States by Japanese terrorists; and Johnny Weismuller, as "Tarzan," triumphed over an evil enemy known as "Nadzies."

Even the normally unflappable Elmer Davis, head of OWI, had to concede the movies were portraying the war all wrong, saying, "Hollywood is letting its imagination carry it away."

That was a gross understatement, according to the writers' division. At first given considerable freedom to write about the war as they saw fit, they now chafed under the heavy hand of the new

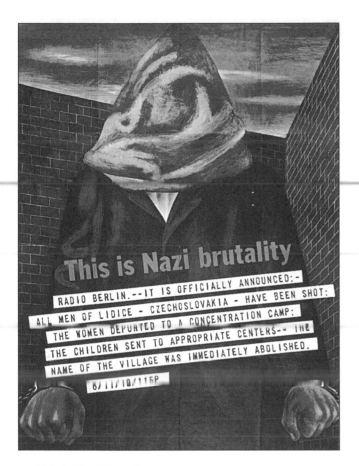

This is Nazi Brutality,
**a poster by OWI artist
Ben Shahn.**

administrators, who included Coca-Cola executives and producers of popular films. The writers had originally been promised the autonomy to collect and disseminate war information according to what they considered to be truthful and vital. Now, however, the new "simple-message" executives at OWI had little use for what the writers had to say.

More than that, the Domestic Branch of OWI was increasingly under assault, accused by Roosevelt's political opponents of being a New Deal agency more intent on promoting the president and his policies than educating the country about the war. Ironically, the writers were struggling in their own thoughtful way to tell the truth about the war, but their ad-men bosses were not backing them. Roosevelt, in turn, did not publicly support either the writers' division or OWI, lest he appear to be manipulating the agency, as his enemies asserted he was.

By April of 1943, OWI's funding from Congress was in jeopardy, and the writers' division was particularly in danger of being cut from the next budget. OWI and its liberal writers were convenient targets for anti-Roosevelt forces in Congress, who wanted to drive home any attack they could against the president. The outspoken writers, although determined not to be anybody's tool, were left out on a limb.

Expressing what many OWI staffers felt, a graphic artist in the agency created a poster image of the Statue of Liberty carrying four bottles of Coca-Cola. The poster — which was never published — bore the slogan "The War that Refreshes: The Four Delicious Freedoms!"

When a grim Ben Shahn poster depicting Nazi brutality was rejected by the new executives, it was clear they preferred Rockwell's

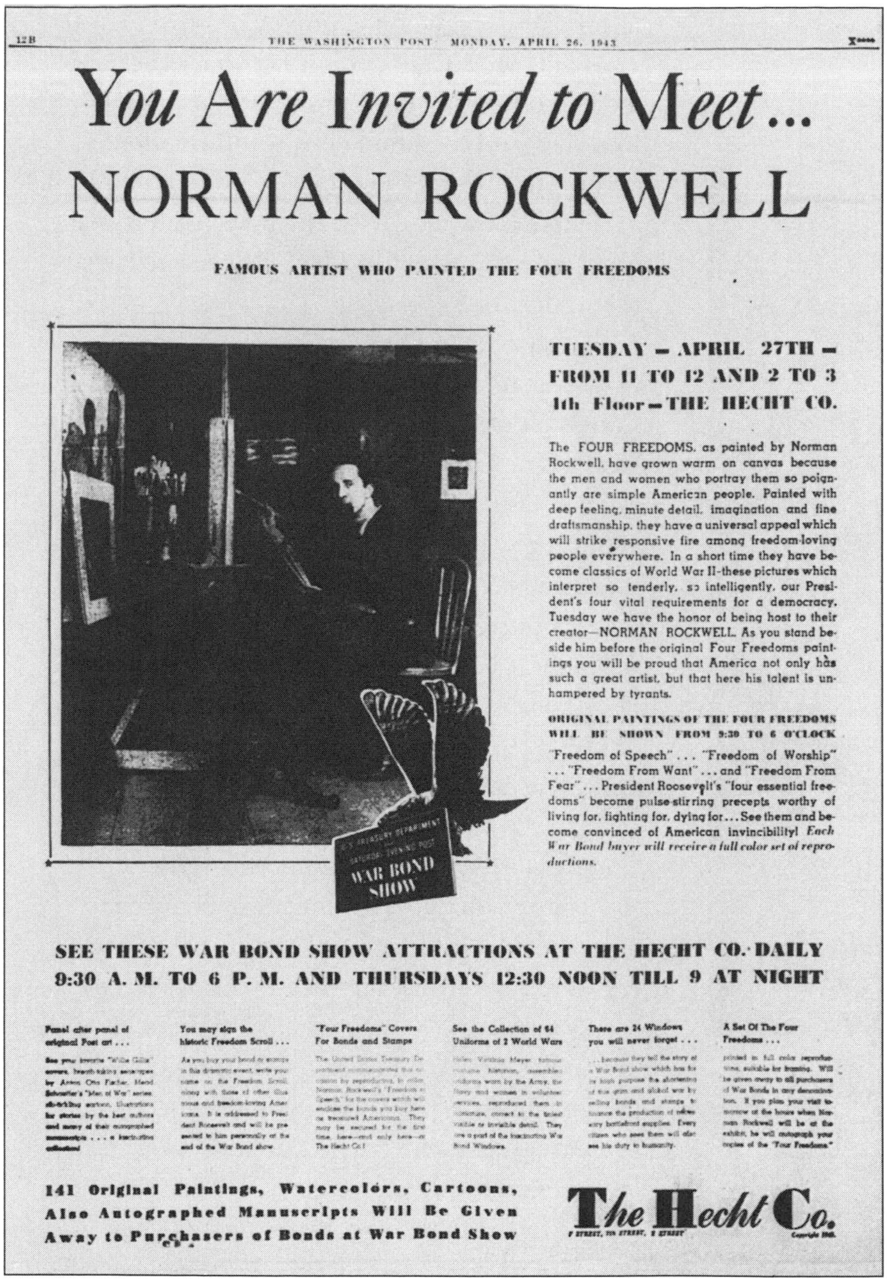

12-B THE WASHINGTON POST: MONDAY, APRIL 26, 1943

You Are Invited to Meet...

NORMAN ROCKWELL

FAMOUS ARTIST WHO PAINTED THE FOUR FREEDOMS

WAR BOND SHOW

TUESDAY — APRIL 27TH — FROM 11 TO 12 AND 2 TO 3 4th Floor—THE HECHT CO.

The FOUR FREEDOMS, as painted by Norman Rockwell, have grown warm on canvas because the men and women who portray them so poignantly are simple American people. Painted with deep feeling, minute detail, imagination and fine draftsmanship, they have a universal appeal which will strike responsive fire among freedom-loving people everywhere. In a short time they have become classics of World War II—these pictures which interpret so tenderly, so intelligently, our President's four vital requirements for a democracy. Tuesday we have the honor of being host to their creator—NORMAN ROCKWELL. As you stand beside him before the original Four Freedoms paintings you will be proud that America not only has such a great artist, but that here his talent is unhampered by tyrants.

ORIGINAL PAINTINGS OF THE FOUR FREEDOMS WILL BE SHOWN FROM 9:30 TO 6 O'CLOCK

"Freedom of Speech" . . . "Freedom of Worship" . . . "Freedom From Want" . . . and "Freedom From Fear" . . . President Roosevelt's "four essential freedoms" become pulse-stirring precepts worthy of living for, fighting for, dying for . . . See them and become convinced of American invincibility! *Each War Bond buyer will receive a full color set of reproductions.*

SEE THESE WAR BOND SHOW ATTRACTIONS AT THE HECHT CO. DAILY 9:30 A. M. TO 6 P. M. AND THURSDAYS 12:30 NOON TILL 9 AT NIGHT

Panel after panel of original Post art . . .

You may sign the historic Freedom Scroll . . .

"Four Freedoms" Covers For Bonds and Stamps

See the Collection of 64 Uniforms of 2 World Wars

There are 24 Windows you will never forget . . .

A Set Of The Four Freedoms . . .

141 Original Paintings, Watercolors, Cartoons, Also Autographed Manuscripts Will Be Given Away to Purchasers of Bonds at War Bond Show

The Hecht Co.

Rockwell was a featured guest at the opening of the Four Freedoms Show in Washington, D.C., at the Hecht Company.

style. The progressive elements of OWI saw this incident as another attempt to impede them; it certainly could not have appealed to the progressives that Rockwell was the most popular illustrator for the conservative *Post*.

The writers' division suffered another blow over a pamphlet it was preparing which warned of a possible nationwide shortage of food in the near future. The Department of Agriculture objected to the pamphlet, even though the text was based on statistics supplied by Agriculture itself. Afraid of giving political ammunition to the powerful farm bloc (which wanted more government financial support at a time when most funding was being channeled to industrial production), Agriculture demanded the writers present, instead, a rosy picture of the food-production situation. When the writers refused, the pamphlet was cancelled by OWI executives and never printed.

The OWI writers were furious, considering this a deliberate falsification of important facts. They resigned en masse just before the April opening of the the Four Freedoms Show to start

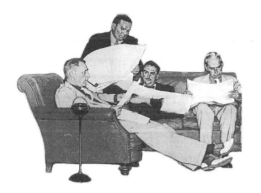

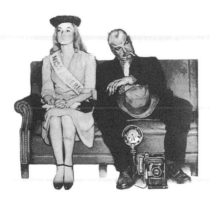

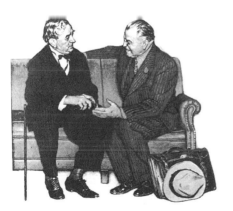

So You Want to See the President: details from Rockwell's series of scenes for the *Post* of the White House front offices.

the war-bond drive. The writers' public statement of resignation said OWI was controlled by "high-pressure promoters who prefer slick salesmanship to honest information. These promoters would treat as stupid and reluctant customers the men and women of the United States."

In the heat of this turmoil within the government's war-information machine, Norman Rockwell's *Four Freedoms* took center stage in Washington, D.C., as the *Post* and Treasury show opened spectacularly at the Hecht Company department store on April 26.

In conjunction with promotional appearances and ceremonies related to the Four Freedoms Show, Rockwell spent a few extra days in Washington making charcoal sketches of people in the waiting rooms of the White House. These were in preparation for illustrations the *Post* planned to run, entitled "So You Want to See the President."

Rockwell not only had to be present at the opening ceremonies at the Hecht Company, but he was the government's guest in the capital city, to be feted and awarded and fashionably seated at places of honor next to wealthy ladies, one of whom thought delightedly that he was the artist Rockwell Kent. Over and over again, Rockwell was beckoned away from the banquet table to be introduced, interviewed, or photographed.

In his autobiography, he said, "I hadn't a chance to drink a cocktail; I wasn't managing to get anything to eat. Someone was always dragging me off to meet ambassadors or other dignitaries. When the oysters came I was called away for photographs. Just as I sank my fork into the capon some reporters demanded my presence."

The next morning, at the show's opening in the Hecht Company store, Rockwell found himself "on a dias in the midst of a churning sea of people" autographing prints of the paintings. The place was stifling and mobbed: "Women in the crowd were fainting; a lady's petticoat dropped around her ankles as she was standing before me — the place resembled Noah's ark on a hot night."

Ironically, another notable should have been sharing the limelight that day, but pointedly chose not to: Treasury Secretary Morgenthau refused an invitation to attend the opening of the Four Freedoms Show. The *Post* had for so long been a staunch opponent of Roosevelt, and relations had been so strained, that Morgenthau said of the magazine, "I wouldn't cross the street for them." Specifically, he objected to a recent article about him, and told his staff, "The *Saturday Evening Post*

Rockwell signed copies of the *Four Freedoms* for bond purchasers at the Hecht Company.

didn't even have the courtesy to show it to me (before publication). It was full of inaccuracies. It just pulls me down."

So it was that Secretary Morgenthau, next to the president the single most important driving force behind the selling of war bonds to the public, did not go to the debut for the Four Freedoms Show to start the second war-bond campaign.

The motto of the show was "Keep the Light of Freedom Burning," and the logo was Liberty's hand and torch. An accompanying art exhibit featured Rockwell's freedoms and showed the works of many other artists and illustrators, such as Mead Schaeffer's series of illustrations depicting the branches of the military, which appeared as *Post* covers. In the exhibit were hundreds of oils, water colors, and cartoons related to the war and to the bond show's theme.

During the run of the Four Freedoms Show at Hecht's there were a number of special events, such as presentations every hour on the hour featuring entertainers, national celebrities, and war heroes, along with films and educational programs. There were booths where war bonds could be purchased, and raffles were held for such items as original *Post* art work and manuscripts.

Each bond purchaser received a set of full-color reproductions of the *Four Freedoms*, and specially designed commemorative covers with *Freedom of Speech* on them held the stamps and bonds bought at the show. Every buyer was invited to sign a list called "The Freedom Scroll," which confirmed one's commitment to the principles behind the four freedoms. At the end of the nationwide tour the scroll was to be presented to President Roosevelt.

As part of the festivities, there were special performances by crack military drill units, choruses sang patriotic songs, and there were exhibits of miniature uniforms from the two world wars. Also on display was a framed and mounted reproduction of the "official" letter from Roosevelt to the *Post* commending the *Four Freedoms* paintings.

News photographers by the score had photo opportunities with dignitaries from Congress, the diplomatic corps, the military, business, and high society. Supreme Court Associate Justice William O. Douglas made the principal address at the show's opening, a program broadcast on radio across the nation, with commentator Lowell Thomas as master of ceremonies.

The Hecht department store, which donated thousands of square feet of floor space for the show, gained much favorable publicity along with an enormous and steady flow of customers who came to shop as well as to see the show. In addition to events in the

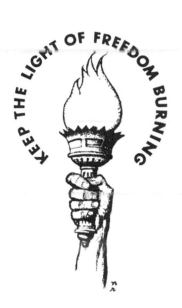

**The logo of the
Four Freedoms War
Bond Show.**

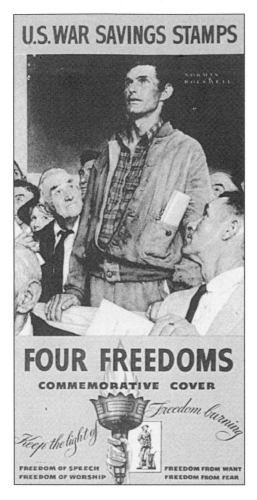

Special *Freedom of Speech* commemorative covers were given to purchasers of war stamps and bonds.

store, there were ceremonies in schools, war plants, and shipyards, and there were citywide rallies and special club luncheons to sell war bonds. Schoolchildren were invited to enter an essay contest on the subject of the four freedoms, and 500 did so.

Throughout the eleven days of the Washington show (it ran through May 8), more than 50,000 persons attended, and more than $1 million in bonds were sold. This pattern of bond sales and patriotic celebration would be followed in fifteen more cities on a year-long itinerary, until the entire country was caught up in the excitement of the Four Freedoms Show.

While he was still in Washington, Norman Rockwell was asked to travel with the show to city after city, but that was the last thing he wanted to do, though he was too polite to come right out and say so. Ben Hibbs well knew Rockwell's feelings and also his reluctance to bluntly refuse to go. So the editor rescued him from embarrassment by publicly declaring that "Norman's going to stay home and do *Post* covers."

The national promotion of the Four Freedoms War Bond Show included what OWI termed "the largest concentration of leading (radio) network shows ever scheduled . . . to carry the Second War Loan message." This involved ninety-one radio programs, selected to reach every segment of the listening audience.

Rockwell, himself, was a guest on several, including NBC's "Lands of the Free" in late February. This was one of a series of broadcasts devoted to the freedoms, and he spoke for four minutes on the subject of freedom of worship. Other speakers in the series were First Lady

Eleanor Roosevelt, *Post* essayist Stephen Vincent Benét, and former OWI official Archibald MacLeish, each of whom also discussed one of the freedoms.

War-bond appeals were heard everywhere, as likely to appear in news broadcasts and women's daytime shows as on "Rudy Vallee," "We, the People in Wartime," the "Camel Comedy Caravan," and "All Time Hit Parade." Symphony and opera broadcasts were also chosen to reach a listener category labeled by OWI as "More Cultured Groups." In the next twelve months, 31,000,000 homes would hear a total of 19,425 bond-drive messages over 925 radio stations.

War-bond appeals also were woven into the scripts of popular radio shows such as those headlined by Burns and Allen, Fibber McGee and Molly, Eddie Cantor, and Jack Benny. Invariably, the message was introduced humorously at first, then the star closed the show with a serious sales pitch. In one, the rich tightwad portrayed by Jack Benny refused to let Rochester, his black chauffeur, borrow the car for a date, Benny using the excuse that because of war shortages he had to save the rubber on the tires.

Rochester replied, "Boss, there ain't no more rubber on the wheels of that car than there is on the Chattanooga Choo-choo." Later, Benny went on to say, earnestly, "When we buy those

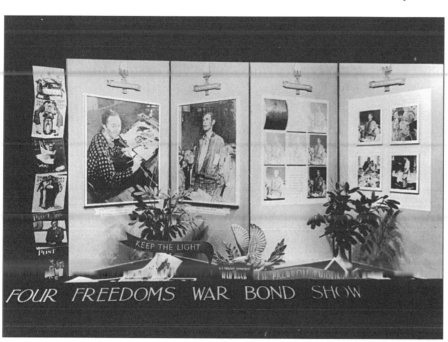

The *Saturday Evening Post* created a series of store window displays for the Four Freedoms War Bond Show.

bonds, remember, we're not doing the *government* a favor. *We're* the government! This is my war, and your war! So let's get rolling . . . hard and fast!"

In addition to radio promotions for war-bond sales, a vast press-release network was employed by OWI, along with editorial cartoons and feature stories created for special newspaper sections. The story of the Second War Loan Drive was even translated into thirty languages for international dissemination. Accompanying all this was a new OWI film entitled "Mission Accomplished," dramatically showing the first bombing of the European continent by American planes. A short trailer with this feature had a soldier asking the theater audience to buy bonds. The bombing film and war-bond trailer were shown simultaneously in 15,000 movie theaters.

As further publicity, OWI arranged for a Paramount News film crew to go Arlington to stage a scene of Rockwell painting the freedoms, using the original models. They were positioned and Rockwell pretended to paint as the cameras whirred to capture a newsreel-length clip. The *Want* models gathered dutifully around the table for the Thanksgiving picture, even though no such overall scene ever had been set up by Rockwell. The *Worship* models were grouped awkwardly in a crowded formation, as they would have been required to stand had Rockwell laboriously painted them this way from life.

Rockwell, of course, had done his work from hundreds of photographs, each specifically set up and illuminated. Yet he good-naturedly went along with OWI's promotion newsreel, which showed him to be merrily at work on the freedoms in his Arlington studio. This would be among the last scenes ever filmed in that studio.

On May 14, Rockwell finished a Boy Scout calendar and sent it off late in the afternoon, before going to a hunting and fishing lecture with Schaeffer. After the lecture, he and some friends met with the speaker back at the studio and enjoyed sociable conversation. The three Rockwell boys were all bundled up in the house, sick with the measles. At 11:30 p.m. the party broke up and Rockwell leaned over the window seat to switch off lights. He did not realize that ashes from his pipe had fallen behind the cushions.

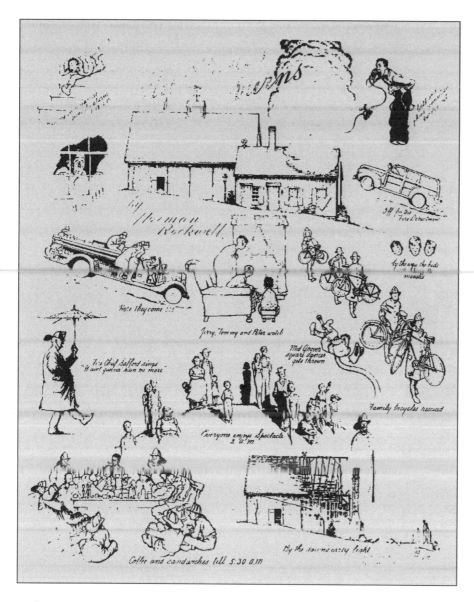

Rockwell recounted the events of his tragic studio fire in a light-hearted series of sketches for the *Post*.

At 1:30 in the morning Rockwell awoke to ten-year-old Tommy banging on the bedroom door and yelling furiously that the studio was on fire. Rockwell sprang to the window and saw it was true: "A storm of flame crackled red and molten gold in the interior of the studio and rolled in a thundering cloud of sparks and smoke through the roof."

The rifle and shotgun shells stored in a drawer in the studio were going off, sending stray bullets zinging through the air. The blaze had knocked out the phone, and by the time Rockwell got his hired man to drive away to rouse the volunteer fire department, it was already too late. Nothing could be done for the studio or the attached barn. Along with firemen, family and neighbors, Rockwell watched helplessly as the studio walls finally crashed in, throwing out a huge, rising shower of sparks "which lit up the mountains across the river, and everybody said, 'Ahhhh,' and fell silent, staring at the fire."

Almost everything Rockwell had collected over a long and successful career was lost — finished paintings, sketches, costumes, resource files, prints, certificates of commendation and awards, even his favorite pipes. He would have to start all over again.

It was strange, he said in his autobiography, but he did not feel sad on that first day after the fire. "Maybe I was in a state of shock."

Initially, he felt most concerned by the loss of his pipes, but friends arrived that very morning, thoughtfully bringing him replacements. The sketches for the White House series also were an important loss, because the *Post* had scheduled a double-page spread, and he had a tight deadline to meet.

It was after returning from a short trip to Washington to make new sketches for this illustration that Rockwell felt the full weight of the disaster. He poked slowly through the ashes of the studio, finding melted guns and the remains of costumes, turning over a lump of lead that must have been his prized pewter mug.

It was "like losing your left arm," he thought, standing where his easel had been. "It gave me an empty feeling in the pit of my stomach."

People and organizations all around the country sympathized with Rockwell's loss. Not only was he given the pipes, but the Society of Illustrators replaced his collection of prints, and Treasury sent a new copy of the citation it had awarded him for the *Four Freedoms*. One of the most moving gestures of kindness came from Mrs. C.A. Palmer of Yakima, Washington, who sent him a palette knife and tile that once had belonged to her mother.

She wrote, "Please accept these trifles with our admiration for you and your work — a fire on top of a war is a bad situation." Mrs. Palmer said her mother had been "a New England girl artist and used these articles in our Montana pioneer home."

Reflecting on the loss, Rockwell soon decided that it had forcibly given him a fresh start on life. He later told an interviewer from the *New Yorker*: "You know, I think it's good for an illustrator to junk everything he has collected once in a while. You get a new viewpoint that way. If you have a lot of pictures filed away you get lazy. You run to your files when you want to see how something looks instead of going out and taking a fresh look."

Mead Schaeffer joked about his friend's positive attitude, saying, "He was so damned convincing that for several weeks I was on the point of burning down my own studio."

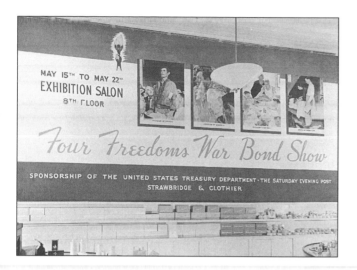

Strawbridge and Clothier in Philadelphia was the second stop of the Four Freedoms Show.

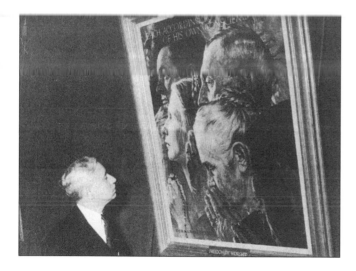

Will Durant, author of the *Post* "Freedom of Worship" essay, was a featured speaker at the Philadelphia Four Freedoms Show.

Talking it over one evening a few days after the fire, Rockwell and Mary decided to move to the nearby hamlet of West Arlington. The very next morning, they bought a house right on the green, across from the Grange and comfortably close to good neighbors. Within days Rockwell was busy equipping a temporary studio in an old one-room schoolhouse that stood on the green beside his new home.

From Washington, D.C., the Four Freedoms War Bond Show traveled to Philadelphia's Strawbridge and Clothier department store, which was coincidentally commemorating its 75th anniversary. Here, the paintings were given a special exhibition room, in a quiet atmosphere with soft background music; this practice was followed in each stop thereafter. Performers Bob Hope and Bing Crosby were special guests, as was author Will Durant, who had written the *Post* essay for "Freedom of Worship." By now, the children's essay contest had 4,000 entries, and more were being eagerly penned in dozens of classrooms in the scheduled cities. On display outside the department store was a 30-ton armored tank. Approximately $881,000 in bonds were sold in Philadelphia.

Momentum already was beginning to grow across the country as the next cities on the itinerary heard news of the bond drive's prior success. Each city sought to find a way to outdo the rest in bond sales and festivities. Community groups of every kind wanted to join in what was shaping up to be a national celebration.

New York was next, the show opening June 4 at Rockefeller Center, and the host was the Fifth Avenue Association of Manhattan businesses. Not to be outdone by Washington or

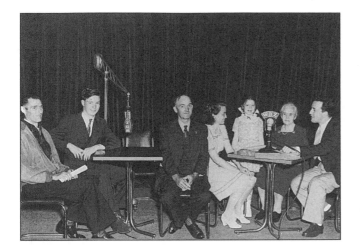

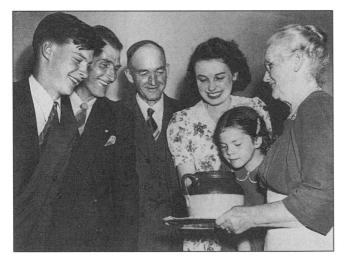

Rockwell's models for the *Four Freedoms* became celebrities themselves, appearing at Filene's in Boston, another stop in the Four Freedoms Show.

They participated in a radio broadcast with a live audience, posed for publicity pictures, and autographed copies of the *Four Freedoms* for bond purchasers.

Philadelphia, New York held a ceremony for the new "Four Freedoms Flag," flown for the first time in conjunction with Flag Day ceremonies. The flag was designed with four upright bars of red on a white background. Singer Kate Smith was featured in the program along with the cast of the new Broadway hit *Oklahoma!* A grim reminder of the war was personified by the appearance of several resolute survivors of the early Philippines defeat.

Attendance at Rockefeller Center was 50,000, with a surprising $13.6 million in bonds sold.

At Filene's department store in Boston, the show opened on June 19, and six of the *Four Freedoms* models came down from Arlington to be featured guests and to sign posters for bond purchasers. The quiet-spoken Carl Hess wore his battered old jacket made famous by *Freedom of Speech*, and answered the questions of local radio interviewers. On a link-up from Vermont, Rockwell joined his models on the radio program.

For little Shirley Hoisington, the girl at the end of the table in *Want*, this was the first long-distance trip of her life. She and the others posed for many photographs, including one of them all looking into a bean pot, the symbol of Boston. She could not understand why they were supposed to look into that pot, because it was empty.

Stacy Holmes, a spokesperson for Filene's, wrote to Rockwell, saying, "It is too bad we could not have made a record of remarks made by visitors as they looked at your paintings. No one could ask for higher praise than the sincere, unrehearsed testimonials of thousands of spectators."

A parade and confetti shower added to the fun, and more than $1.6 million in bonds were sold. Bostonians were pleased that the sales total was larger than both Washington and Philadelphia, and that the number of transactions was greater than New York's.

Moving to Buffalo, New York, on July 12, the show became linked with the large ethnic communities of the region — as would happen all throughout the Midwest tour. The entertainment included traditional folk music and dance, in particular from Buffalo's Polish organizations. The host store was the William Hengerer Company, where bond buyers paid out $582,000, which symbolically purchased four fighter-bombers, each given the name of a freedom.

In Rochester, New York, the show opened on August 2, and for the first time featured demonstrations of a working war-plant assembly line, set up in Sibley, Linday and Curr, the sponsoring store. Here, also for the first time, Rockwell's paintings were accompanied by controlled lighting and recorded explanations of the meaning of the four freedoms. More than 72,000 attended, raising $901,000.

The Pittsburgh show held in Kaufmann's department store and beginning on September 8, also included presentations and support from many ethnic groups, who organized parades, sold bonds from their own special booths, and sponsored the purchase of military equipment. Almost $7.8 million in war bonds were sold.

On September 26, while the show was touring, a symphony entitled "The Four Freedoms" and composed by Robert Russell Bennett was performed in New York by the NBC Symphony Orchestra at Radio City. The symphony was inspired by Rockwell's paint-

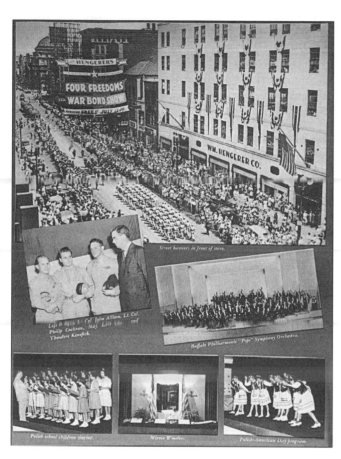

The William Hengerer Company in Buffalo sponsored a variety of events for the Four Freedoms Show, as illustrated in a page from the show's Summary Report.

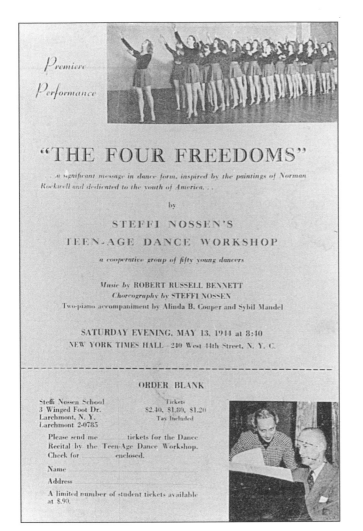

A symphony by Robert Russell Bennett was inspired by Rockwell's *Four Freedoms*, and was also choreographed.

ings, according to Bennett, who said he "tried to follow the pictures as a motion picture score follows the idea of the film." Part of the ongoing national celebration of the freedoms, this premiere performance was broadcast across the country.

That night Rockwell sent a complimentary telegram to Bennett at Radio City, saying, "I am more than deeply impressed with your significant contribution to these times . . . [and] its complete fidelity to the spirit underlying the Four Freedoms themselves."

Also inspired by Rockwell's paintings, and choreographed to the music of the Bennett symphony, was a dance created in 1944 by Steffi Nossen's Dance Workshop.

The J.L. Hudson Company in Detroit next sponsored the Four Freedoms Show, which opened on September 27 and was marked by a parade through the city that was viewed by more than 300,000 people. Elements of the show went to war plants and football games, and the show raised more than $2.7 million.

Cleveland was next, on October 25, at May Company. Here, vice president Henry Wallace put in a guest appearance, and $589,000 in bond sales was achieved.

At Chicago's Carson Pirie Scott Company, the show opened November 11 and had as its theme "Beat New York." This drive was tremendously successful, with more than $17 million in bond sales, the record to date. Enormous rallies were held, and a massive advertising campaign was run, distributing promotional flyers and posters throughout the city to churches, in taxicabs, delivered with milk bottles, and given out with bank statements and gasoline receipts. The eleven-day Chicago show coincided with

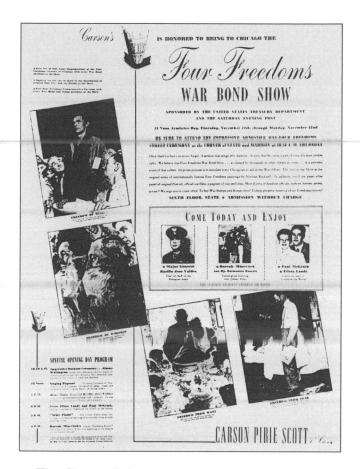

The *Chigago Tribune* advertised the events at the Carson Pirie Scott Company's Four Freedoms Show.

PRIVILEGES

FREEDOM OF SPEECH
★
FREEDOM OF WORSHIP
★
FREEDOM FROM WANT
★
FREEDOM FROM FEAR

These FOUR FREEDOMS are America's most precious possessions. They will be preserved through the combined efforts of our Commander-in-Chief and his staff, the men in our armed forces and the people on the home front who are furnishing our fighting men with munitions of war through the purchase of War Bonds.

The people of Chicago are cordially invited to attend the exhibition of Norman Rockwell's famous original paintings, depicting the FOUR FREEDOMS, at Carson Pirie Scott & Company. These magnificent paintings will be on display from November 11 through November 22, under the sponsorship of the United States Treasury Department, The Saturday Evening Post and Carson Pirie Scott & Company.

BUY MORE WAR BONDS

A variety of business corporations supported advertisements about the four freedoms ideals and the Four Freedoms Show.

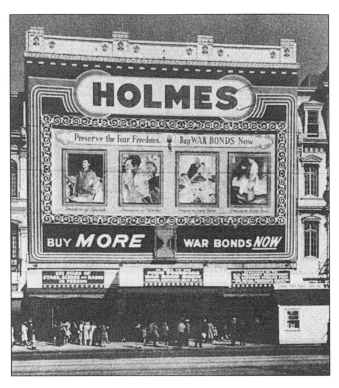

A sixty-foot painted sign of Rockwell's *Four Freedoms* was displayed on the Holmes department store in New Orleans, one of the stops of the Four Freedoms Show.

the commemoration of Armistice Day, and guests included film stars Rita Hayworth and Orson Welles.

State chairman of the War Finance Committee, Harold H. Swift, said that "the whole city of Chicago was thrilled by the paintings and made more conscious of our war aims."

The St. Louis show at Stix, Baer and Fuller began December 16 and ran through the holiday shopping season, with the theme "Four Freedoms Christmas." Democratic Congressman J. William Fulbright of Arkansas, recognized as a specialist in understanding and teaching of U.S. foreign policy, was the keynote speaker. The show raised $4.3 million.

On January 16, 1944, in New Orleans, the show was sponsored by the Retail Merchants Association and held in the Municipal Auditorium. It became a huge community effort, with schools being let out early, canvassers selling bonds door-to-door, and — typical for New Orleans, birthplace of jazz — eighteen lively brass bands appeared in the parade. On the front of Holmes, a sponsoring department store, was a sixty-foot painted sign showing Rockwell's *Four Freedoms*. New Orleans set the single-show record up to that time, with $21.3 million in bond sales.

At Tisch-Goettinger Company in Dallas, the show opened on January 27, and was visited by 75,000 people. Raising $6.2 million, it featured an appearance by Gwen Dew, a news correspondent who for a time had been a captive of the Japanese.

Traveling to Los Angeles on February 12, the show was sponsored by Bullock's, and a "Hollywood Spectacle" was the main event.

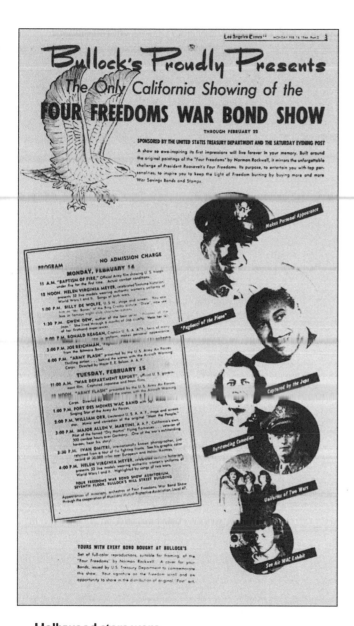

Hollywood stars were featured at the Four Freedoms Show hosted by Bullock's in Los Angeles.

Many motion picture stars now in uniform were featured in personal appearances, and there were more than 100,000 visitors. More than $22 million in bonds was sold, setting the record, but not for long.

Portland, Oregon, was the home of War Finance Division Director Theodore Gamble, who ran the entire war-bond operation for the Treasury. Beginning on March 27, the Portland show recorded the largest bond sale total of all: $31.2 million. Sponsored by Meier & Frank, this was another huge community event. It also featured several survivors of the Philippines campaign, men who had come through the infamous Bataan "Death March."

Aaron M. Frank, president of the department store, said "The *Saturday Evening Post* deserves the thanks of the entire nation for having the foresight to realize the possibilities of Norman Rockwell's original paintings of the four freedoms."

On May 1-8, 1944, a year after it began, the Four Freedoms War Bond Show ended its tour at Denver Dry Goods, Denver, where a worldwide broadcast was sent out on network radio and on short-wave by OWI. Comedian Bob Hope was the main celebrity, and $912,000 was raised.

At every city on the Four Freedoms Show tour, the ambitious organization of festivities and events was in large part carried out by volunteers. It is remarkable that no written agreements were ever signed. By the end of the tour, more than 1.2 million people had seen the show, almost $133 million in war bonds were sold, and at least 450 celebrities had put in appearances at the ceremonies.

In a public statement about the Four Freedoms Show, Treasury Secretary Morgenthau said, "Here is a picture of democracy at work in its hour of crisis. The retailers of the country are to be congratulated for sponsoring this community-wide event. . . . Norman Rockwell's paintings, the *Four Freedoms*, are dramatic illustrations of the principles for which we fight. The number of E-bonds sold proves the success of the show in reaching the average citizen."

The images of Rockwell's *Four Freedoms* were to be seen everywhere in those days. OWI eventually printed four million sets of posters, some for war-bond buyers and the rest for display in schools, post offices, railroad stations, houses of worship, social clubs, hotels, government offices, and even poolrooms. In addition to this vast distribution of the *Freedoms*, the *Post* gave permission to a large number of publications and businesses to reprint them for their own purposes.

It has been said that no graphic images ever have been reproduced in such numbers. While this is perhaps impossible to confirm, certainly Norman Rockwell's *Four Freedoms* are among the most widely reproduced and most famous paintings of all time.

President Franklin Delano Roosevelt died suddenly on April 12, 1945, the eve of the surrender of Nazi Germany to the United Nations. Those who loved Roosevelt and saw him as a great leader of the country and the world were profoundly sorrowful, among them Samuel Rosenman, the writer who had witnessed the birth of the Four Freedoms speech in 1941.

In his memoirs, Rosenman said, "The four freedoms were not presented by Roosevelt as something from on high; instead he spoke of them in terms of the desires and needs of all human beings in the world, and each person who heard the President talk about them could feel: 'Yes, that's what I'd like to see happen myself.'"

After the war, as the reorganized United Nations was established in a world desperate for lasting peace, many national leaders agreed that people of all countries had an inalienable right to the four freedoms. In 1945, Eleanor Roosevelt was appointed by President Harry S. Truman as a delegate to the U.N., where she was chairwoman of the Commission on Human Rights from 1946-51. In this capacity, Mrs. Roosevelt was instrumental in winning the General Assembly's adoption, in 1948, of the "Universal

Declaration of Human Rights." Based on the principles of the four freedoms, this declaration became part of the U.N.'s "International Bill of Rights," which was a cornerstone in the organization's founding charter.

The legacy of the Roosevelt four freedoms also continues through the Franklin and Eleanor Roosevelt Institute, which presents the "Four Freedoms Awards" to men and women who, in some outstanding manner, have worked for the ideals expressed in them. Long after World War II, many people still associate Roosevelt with the four basic human freedoms that he articulated so well for them.

As Samuel Rosenman put it, "Each person in the great masses of people all over the world felt that here was a man who was fighting not only *for* him, but *with* him: fighting for some peace and security . . . for some better food and shelter and clothing for him and his family."

In some ways, it was the same with Norman Rockwell. People who saw his paintings considered him to be one of them. They comprehended the stories he told without words, and recognized the characters he portrayed — characters much like them, like their relations and friends.

"He understands us," they said, and felt they understood him in return.

The burning of Rockwell's Arlington studio in 1943 was literally a break with the past. He lost all he had collected in thirty years as an illustrator and had to begin all over. Both his life and career were jolted by the experience.

In his autobiography, Rockwell described this period as "I Rise from the Ashes," which is a characteristic understatement. In fact, the decade during and after World War II saw Rockwell produce many examples of other serious work, such as *The Long Shadow of Lincoln*, published on February 10, 1945, to illustrate a story by Carl Sandburg. The painting portrays the peoples of America and the world grouped around a disabled soldier, as they prepare to rebuild after the war. Some look toward the future, some pray.

Other paintings from this period that captured the details of changing society include *Homecoming Marine* (1945), *County*

Agricultural Agent (1948), *Shuffleton's Barber Shop* (1950), and *Saying Grace* (1951). His images were more than ever depictions of the human condition — the human condition as he chose to view it.

In *Saying Grace* an old woman and a child pray at a table in a shabby railroad restaurant while other customers look on. Rockwell wrote that in real life some people might have been rude or insulting to the woman and child.

"But I didn't see it that way. I just naturally made the people respectful. The picture is not absolutely true to life; it's not a photograph of an actual scene but the scene as I saw it."

Scenes of the human condition as Rockwell saw it stayed prominent in the public eye year after year, for the *Post* continued to employ him in its quest to be an immediate and timely reflection of life in America. Springing from out of World War II work such as *Night on a Troop Train* and *So You Want to See the President*, Rockwell's art nowadays was often almost reportage. This was especially true of the well-loved *Post* series entitled "Norman Rockwell Visits." These included paintings of scenes at a country newspaper, a family doctor's office, a maternity ward, and a country school.

By 1953 the Rockwells felt the need to be in less isolated surroundings and they moved from Arlington to Stockbridge, Massachusetts. In his autobiography, Rockwell described himself as "restless again. And then I was having trouble with my work and thought that maybe a change would help me." They maintained their friendships with Vermont neighbors, but the little group of brilliant illustrators, who through the forties had worked and raised families together, broke up, all going their separate ways.

The early years in Stockbridge are noteworthy for some of Rockwell's best known and most admired paintings, among them *Breaking Home Ties* (1954) and *Marriage License* (1955). In this period he painted portraits of President Dwight D. Eisenhower and unsuccessful presidential candidate Adlai E. Stevenson; he also painted portraits of presidential candidates Richard M. Nixon and John F. Kennedy.

Then, in the summer of 1959, Mary died unexpectedly. It was an agonizing loss to Rockwell, whose only solace was to keep on working. He painted a portrait of Mary for the dedication page of his autobiography, which was published in 1960, and produced *Triple Self-Portrait* to accompany the first installment of the book in the *Post*.

Thomas Rockwell later wrote: "He handled his grief partly by working in spite of it; his work was the structure of his life."

After the 1943-44 war-bond show, the *Four Freedoms* paintings and the related exhibit had again traveled for some months around the country, this time by train, in a custom-made car. The phenomenal popular success of the show and this train inspired the 1947-48 "Freedom Train," which toured the country with an exhibit of historic documents.

The sleek new "Streamliner" was called "The Spirit of 1776," and it visited all forty-eight states, carrying 132 documents, including a letter written by Christopher Columbus in 1493, the Declaration of Independence, George Washington's personal copy of the Constitution, and Lincoln's Gettysburg Address. This train did not have the original Rockwell paintings — they appeared in publications distributed as part of the program — but there was another "Freedom Scroll" for viewers to sign and so to affirm their dedication to liberty and democracy.

More than 3.5 million visitors saw the "Freedom Train" exhibit in 326 cities. The idea for the exhibit is said to have come from an official in the Justice Department who had earlier worked with the war-bond show.

Throughout the 1950s the *Four Freedoms* paintings hung in the offices of Post editor Ben Hibbs, who so loved them. Hibbs retired as editor in 1961, at the beginning of the end of the venerable old *Post*. By the time the magazine closed up in 1969, Norman Rockwell had recovered the original paintings and kept them at his home in Stockbridge.

In 1961, Rockwell married Molly Punderson, who had grown up in Stockbridge and was the leader of a poetry class he attended. "Everyone was pleased," Thomas Rockwell recalled.

Molly traveled with her husband on extensive magazine assignments that took them all around the world. On a trip to Moscow, Rockwell brought the *Four Freedoms* originals along, and they were placed on public exhibit as part of a cultural exchange program with the United States.

Through the sixties, Rockwell painted mostly for *Look* magazine, and now his work was not only journalistic, but it dealt with controversial social subjects, from race relations to education to the government's declared "war on poverty." His strong belief in the equality of mankind can be seen in *The Golden Rule* (1961), which was inspired by the ideals of the United Nations. This painting was an outgrowth of an earlier attempt — like the attempt which produced the *Four Freedoms* — to create "the BIG picture," as he wrote in his autobiography.

"I sincerely wanted to do a picture which would help the world out of the mess it's in, and as it seemed to me that the United Nations was our only hope . . . I decided to do a picture of a scene at the U.N."

While still living in Arlington, Rockwell had begun but never completed a

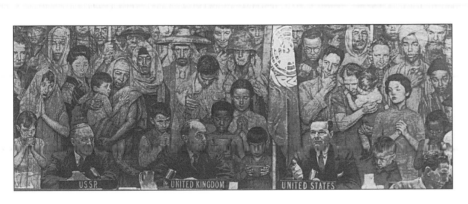

A portrayal of the United Nations Security Council chamber by Rockwell.

grand view of the U.N. Security Council chamber, with several delegates in the foreground and a host of ordinary people intently looking on behind them. For a number of reasons, Rockwell never completed this "big picture" effort, but *Golden Rule* more than ten years later was the outcome of his preparatory work.

A similar frontal composition of a group of people is found in *The Right to Know* (1968), with individuals facing the viewer across a judge's bench. Compositions that were first developed in the *Four Freedoms* are used in a number of Rockwell works from the sixties. The artist's admiration of Kennedy is apparent in a 1966 story illustration, *JFK's Bold Legacy*, showing a grouping similar to that in *Freedom of Worship*: closeups in profile of a visionary Kennedy and several intent young people, who were Peace Corps volunteers.

Rockwell eventually responded to that 1943 plea for him to address civil rights, when he painted a black child breaking the color line in *The Problem We All Live With* (1964). Another related image, that of civil rights workers facing imminent death in *Southern Justice* (1965), is a sharp departure from Rockwell's more gentle treatment of the human condition, but once again the illustrator deftly and lucidly captures a telling moment in American life — as he saw it.

In 1967, Norman and Molly Rockwell helped the Stockbridge Historical Society purchase a colonial house on Main Street, converting it first into a historical museum and also exhibiting some of Rockwell's originals there. "The Old Corner House," as it was named, attracted thousands of visitors each year, growing steadily in importance until it became known as "The Norman Rockwell Museum at The Old Corner House."

For almost twenty-five years the *Four Freedoms* remained on exhibit at The Old Corner House along with many other original Rockwells. In that time, more than two million visitors came from all over the United States and scores of countries from around the world. For many, the *Four Freedoms* are the most memorable Rockwell paintings of all.

In 1973, Rockwell established a trust to preserve his artistic legacy and placed it under the custodianship of the museum. Though weakening physically after two serious falls, he continued to paint for a few more years — in fact he was offered more commissions than he ever could have completed.

Rockwell's final cover illustration was executed for *American Artist* magazine's 1976 commemoration of the nation's bicentennial. He painted himself jauntily draping a "Happy Birthday" ribbon on the Liberty Bell.

On November 8, 1978, at the age of 84, Norman Rockwell died peacefully at his home in Stockbridge, an unfinished painting on his easel.

In 1983, the Rockwell museum acquired Linwood, a thirty-six-acre Victorian estate outside Stockbridge village, and began the process of constructing a new gallery building to house its collection of more than 500 Rockwell originals and thousands of artifacts and archives that belonged to the artist.

Rockwell's Stockbridge studio was moved to the Linwood grounds in 1986, where it now overlooks the winding Housatonic River. Nearby is the gallery building of the Norman Rockwell Museum at Stockbridge, which opened in 1993, in time for the fiftieth anniversary of the publishing of the *Four Freedoms*. The museum includes 7,500 square feet of exhibit space as well as classrooms, an auditorium, a library, studios, and extensive archival storage. The museum is designed in the tradition of a New England meeting house, with a graceful windowed cupola to let light fall into the central gallery.

When the new museum opened, hanging in that gallery beneath the cupola were Norman Rockwell's four most famous paintings: *Freedom of Speech*, *Freedom of Worship*, *Freedom from Want*, and *Freedom from Fear*.

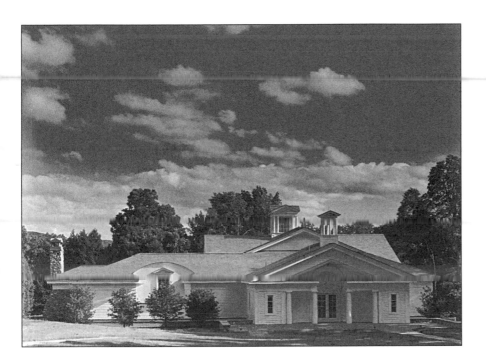

Rockwell's *Four Freedoms* are now exhibited in the Norman Rockwell Museum at Stockbridge.

Rockwell's speaker stands relaxed and confident, a Lincolnesque figure in working clothes. His argument is compelling. Two men in suits, perhaps his economic betters, turn and listen intently as a young girl shyly casts an admiring glance. They discuss a report on an unknown subject, Americans of all ages gathering in modest surroundings to fulfill the American promise of free speech and assembly.

Would Rockwell paint a different image today, fifty years later? Yes and no. Democracy is never fixed, it is never certain, never secure. Our notions of freedom and justice evolve and thus, were Rockwell to paint today, the speaker might be a woman and the crowd certainly would reflect America with all its hues and colors, races, and religions. Rockwell might show more ambiguity in the faces of the listeners, or even outright disagreement, since today we have no clearly evil foe such as Hitler, and our world is more complex and baffling.

Franklin Roosevelt, when he proclaimed the Four Freedoms, said, "Those who would give up essential liberty to purchase a little temporary safety, deserve neither liberty nor safety." Speech is bold and resolute — a state of mind in which there is no urge to be secure, no concession to the intimidators, and no fear of the consequences. So Roosevelt proclaimed it. So Rockwell painted it. And so it remains.

Three of the four freedoms that Roosevelt identified and Rockwell painted come from our First Amendment: speech, worship, and freedom from fear. The First Amendment, in turn, acknowledges that these freedoms inherently belong to us as citizens and Congress shall not limit them. But the concept of free speech means nothing if it protects only that speech with which we agree. Speech is the tool by which we hammer out the clauses in our social contract, generation by generation. We don't reach that consensus by prohibiting those ideas with which we disagree, and thus the answer to offensive or contentious speech is always more speech — persuasive speech.

If we lose our freedom, it will be because we have let it slip away in small increments. It will die a little when it is too much trouble to go to the school board meeting to challenge well-meaning parents who seek to ban books from the school library. It will erode when we scream at our congressional representatives to ban difficult or confrontational art. It will be tarnished when speech codes are accepted on college campuses.

Rockwell's speaker is standing up, an act of courage and participation. Speech, like a muscle, grows stronger with use and atrophies with inactivity. And while some may say that contentious speech is a price we must pay for a democracy, I believe that both Roosevelt and Rockwell would portray it as democracy's reward.

Freedom of Worship
Theodore H. Evans

Among the oldest artifacts of human civilization are those which indicate that people have always responded to something beyond physical reality — to experiences of the holy, the wholly other, the divine. Worship, literally, worth-ship, means the ascribing of worth, of ultimate value. We worship that which we most value and what we believe to be the source of our meaning and purpose.

Human response to ultimate value takes many forms. It can be as elaborate and mysterious as a pontifical high mass, accompanied by music, incense, and processions, and presided over by clergy in richly adorned vestments. It can be as simple as the daily meditations of a Buddhist priest or the peaceful quiet of a meeting for worship of the Community of Friends. Muslim worshipers respond to the call to prayer by bowing toward the holy city of Mecca and reciting part of the Quran. Hasidic Jews cover their shoulders with prayer shawls when they gather for morning prayers and to read the Holy Scriptures. Liturgical and ecstatic dance, chant, and even animal sacrifice have been among the many ways people have acted out their response to the divine presence.

Norman Rockwell's illustration of the second of President Franklin Delano Roosevelt's Four Freedoms, the freedom of religion, is an image of the faces of many people. Each represents a different race, culture, or religious tradition. The faces are rendered in grayish hues suggesting, perhaps, the great variety and, at the same time, the fundamental similarity of the human spirit's response in worship to that which the world's religions have known and experienced as ultimate.

Freedom of worship, both as it was proclaimed by President Roosevelt and imaged on canvas by Norman Rockwell, affirms a pluralistic approach to religion and culture that respects, encourages, and protects the forms, customs, liturgies, and beliefs of all religious traditions, and of no religious tradition at all. In its particular time in history it declared the hope and the belief that the world should be free of racial discrimination, from religious persecution, and from dictators and totalitarian states that would require or try to require total obedience — even worship of them. (How thrilling it is that we have recently learned since the Iron Curtain's fall what we should have known all along, that religion and worship never ceased even in the most repressive anti-religion regimes!) That there should be such freedom in our world and in our land was and is a worthy intention, but not one that is free from difficulties.

Worship and ethics are inseparable. The way we live our lives is an expression of our worship and demonstrates more clearly than all our words what we truly value. It is this aspect of worship that can and often does cause conflict. A religious majority may impose or try to impose its special values on a whole society. A vocal, highly organized, and motivated minority can do the same. In the name of religion the most terrible atrocities have been and are still being committed. There have been too many examples in recent years not to recognize the dark side of religious freedom.

Like all true freedoms, the freedom of worship carries necessary responsibilities. Justice Holmes is reported to have said on the subject of the relativity of freedom, "The freedom for a man to swing his fist leaves off where the other man's nose begins." Similarly, when the exercise of our freedom of worship moves us, as it must, into the realms of public policy and personal behavior, we need to be especially vigilant and sensitive to the necessity to be tolerant of other perspectives and points of view and to remain open to the possibility of change — even our own.

Freedom of worship like democracy itself will never be absolute. It remains a goal whose approaching requires the persistent and cooperative attention of us all. Roosevelt's speech and Rockwell's image provide visions of a world in which differences matter less than our common humanity and where variety is valued and affirmed. It remains for us to work toward realization of their visions.

Freedom from Want
James MacGregor Burns

Of all his *Four Freedom* portraits, Norman Rockwell's *Freedom from Want* probably aroused in Americans their warmest, happiest memories. Who could forget that huge turkey in the center of the picture, the benign older couple still serving as nurturing grandparents, the excited, happy faces of young and old around the table? For millions of others who might some day see it, of course, — black and yellow and brown people around the globe — the happy white, middle-class family and its bountiful food reminded them of just what they lacked — and what they wanted.

Franklin D. Roosevelt well knew of this want, in America and around the world. He had taken office in 1933 at a time when ten million or more Americans lacked jobs, and millions more lacked adequate food and shelter and clothing. Even so, freedom from want did not seem to lie so heavily in his mind in 1940 as the other three freedoms. When a reporter asked him in July of that year to spell out his long-range peace aims, Roosevelt slowly listed them: freedom of information and of religion and of self-expression and freedom from fear.

Wasn't there a fifth freedom, a reporter asked — freedom from want? Yes, he had forgotten it, Roosevelt said. Perhaps this was because want was only too familiar to him while he was exploring the reach of the other freedoms.

Certainly he did not neglect freedom from want when, in January 1941, he spelled out the Four Freedoms to Congress. After mentioning freedom of religion and speech he came to a third freedom — "freedom from want — which, translated into world terms, means economic understandings which will secure to every nation a healthy peacetime life for its inhabitants — everywhere in the world."

That Roosevelt had a concrete sense of this freedom became immediately apparent in this same speech when he spelled out what came to be known as an "economic bill of rights":

Equality of opportunity for youth and for others;
Jobs for those who can work;
Security for those who need it;
The ending of special privilege for the few;
The preservation of civil liberties for all;

The enjoyment of the fruits of scientific progress in a wider and constantly rising standard of living.

During the following years Roosevelt made freedom from want even more concrete by expanding his economic bill of rights. He spoke to the nation about the need for better housing, more hospitals, of more highways, parkways, and airports, of health clinics and new cheap automobiles.

So dramatically did Roosevelt pitch the need for freedom from want — and especially doing so in global terms — that his economic bill of rights served as a foundation for United States economic policy at home and abroad for decades following his death and the end of World War II. At home the economic bill of rights virtually made up the agenda not only of Democratic candidates and administrations but to a considerable extent of the Republican as well, beginning with Dwight Eisenhower. Satisfying human wants was the very foundation also of the Marshall Plan and its successors in Europe, and of many Third and Fourth World economic aid and investment programs. Thus human want had become converted into legitimate need, which in turn served as the guide to policy.

All this would have immensely pleased the author of the Four Freedoms. For he was not only unparalleled in his ability to invent and enunciate policy; he was even more concerned about translating oratory into the satisfying of people's concrete wants, especially hunger — not excluding the hearty appetites of those gathered around a Thanksgiving dinner table!

Freedom from Fear
Brian Urquhart

Franklin Delano Roosevelt's Four Freedoms speech, on January 6, 1941, illuminated the darkest years of the Second World War with his vision of a world founded upon four freedoms — freedom of speech, freedom of worship, freedom from want, and freedom from fear. Long before the war had ended — even before victory was assured — Roosevelt had turned his attention to the essential principles and foundations of the future peace. He believed that freedom from fear, an inseparable part of the other freedoms, could only be achieved in a world without war, a world of well-distributed prosperity with equal justice, equal opportunities, and equal rights for all its inhabitants.

In the fifty years that have passed since Roosevelt's great declaration, the world has changed faster and in more fundamental ways than at any other time in recorded history. The age of empires has ended; democracy is gaining ground; the population has doubled and is still increasing rapidly; technology is changing the way in which people think, work, and communicate with each other; and a great new range of global problems has emerged, problems which no single nation can resolve on its own.

Our world is now less a prey to monstrous and vicious tyrannies, but it is, as yet, by no means free from fear. Although freedom and human rights are almost universally accepted as indispensable attributes of the human race, fear, and a pervading sense of insecurity, are still widespread.

The fear that now weighs upon so many people is not the desperate terror inspired by the secret police of a ruthless dictator or the panic that descends on civilians caught in a war zone. It is something deeper and longer-lasting — fear of poverty, of hunger and disease, of being unable to survive or complete; fear, even, of the future itself. In a world in which nearly a third of the population lives below the poverty line such fears are very common.

More fortunate people also have deep and imprecise fears. They fear the decay of the familiar supports of society, the increasing threats to the life-sustaining environment, and the unpredictable results of racial or ethnic hatred and resentment. They fear the inhuman scale of the technology of modern industrial society and the perversion of its uses. They fear the weapons of mass destruction which the chaotic conditions of some parts of the world may well deliver into the wrong hands. They fear insecurity of all kinds.

The only effective way to dispel fear is to attack its causes. We have recently discovered that for all our knowledge and expertise, we are living in a world of great uncertainty. Only by facing up to problems, combining our efforts to find the right answers and acting upon them, shall we regain our confidence and our sense of purpose, our pride in human destiny. The obstacles are enormous, but so, after all, were the challenges which inspired Roosevelt, in his first Inaugural speech, to tell the people of the United States, "We have nothing to fear but fear itself."

The Four Freedoms
William J. vanden Heuvel

We look back in order to see where we are going. We need only remember the world to which Franklin Roosevelt spoke on January 6, 1941, to be reminded of the blessings of our lives today. The world then — beset by war, oppressed by Nazi domination, brutalized by racist thugs — was a world where every tenet of democracy was threatened and ridiculed. The Four Freedoms bring the past and present together. They are the freedoms for which we fought; they are the words inscribed in the Charter of the United Nations and the Universal Declaration of Human Rights; they are the fundamental values of the world we would leave to our children.

On January 6, 1941, President Roosevelt came before the Congress and gave us a vision of the world that would be worthy of our civilization. He spoke — simply, eloquently — of a nation dedicated to the Four Freedoms — everywhere in the world:

Freedom of speech and expression, the best defense against the corruption of democracy;

Freedom of worship, our shield against the forces of bigotry, intolerance, and fanaticism;

Freedom from want, a commitment to erasing hunger, poverty, and pestilence from the earth;

Freedom from fear, a freedom dependent on collective security, a concept carried forward with our leadership in the United Nations.

The words and concepts of the Four Freedoms were distinctly personal to President Roosevelt. He wrote the phrases himself, he spoke them deliberately and simply to explain to the American people that their history of isolation was over, that the United States had no choice but to commit its enormous power to defeat the Fascist dictators. Franklin Roosevelt wanted not only his countrymen but every nation in the world to understand that the Four Freedoms justified the battle, made worthy the sacrifice, made essential the victory.

Who was this leader of whom Winston Churchill said, "He is the greatest man I have ever known"?

Franklin Roosevelt was the voice of the people of the United States during the most difficult crises of the century. He led America out of the despair of the Great Depression. He led us to victory in World War II. Four times he was elected President of the United States. By temperament and talent, by energy and instinct, Franklin

Roosevelt was ready for the challenges that confronted him. He was a breath of fresh air in our political life — so vital, so confident and optimistic, so warm and good-humored. He was a man of incomparable personal courage. He is the only person in recorded history chosen as leader of his people even though he could not walk or stand without help. At the age of 39, he had been stricken with infantile paralysis. The pain of his struggle is almost unimaginable — learning to move again, to stand, to rely upon the physical support of others — never giving into despair, to self-pity, to discouragement. He gave that courage to his country at a time of its greatest need. He replaced fear with faith, transforming our government into an active instrument of social justice.

It was a time when heroes were possible, when idealism was admired, when public service was the highest calling. It was also a time when Adolf Hitler laid claim to the future. President Roosevelt warned the world to quarantine the aggressors. He made America the arsenal of democracy. He was Commander-in-Chief of the greatest military force in history. He crafted the victorious alliance that won the war. He was the father of the nuclear age. He guided the blueprint for the world that was to follow. The vision of the United Nations, the commitment to collective security, the determination to end colonialism, the economic plan for a prosperous world with access to resources and trade assured to all nations — such was the legacy of Franklin Roosevelt.

The Cold War blocked the fulfillment of his dreams for a better world. Now it is over. We witness disappointed expectations. We see agonizing struggles between ancient rivals. Some question whether the democracies can meet the challenge.

We need the patience to prevail, the discipline to succeed, the courage to accept the challenge. The Four Freedoms have never been more relevant.

A newspaper editor in Kansas, hearing the Four Freedoms speech in January, 1941, declared that "the people of the United States through their President have given the world a new Magna Carta of democracy." "The Four Freedoms," said William Allen White, "mark the opening of a new era for the world. A great occasion, a great cause and a great man have been united."

The editor from Kansas was right. President Roosevelt's words live on, and each succeeding generation must take hold of this dream, understand it, believe in it, work for it, and go forth with new strength and purpose in our commitment to freedom.

The four freedoms of common humanity are as much elements of man's needs as air and sunlight, bread and salt. Deprive him of all these freedoms and he dies — deprive him of a part of them and a part of him withers. Give them to him in full and abundant measure and he will cross the threshold of a new age, the greatest age of man.

These freedoms are the rights of men of every creed and every race, wherever they live. This is their heritage, long withheld. We of the United Nations have the power and the men and the will at last to assure man's heritage.

The belief in the four freedoms of common humanity — the belief in man, created free, in the image of God — is the crucial difference between ourselves and the enemies we face today. In it lies the absolute unity of our alliance, opposed to the oneness of the evil we hate. Here is our strength, the source and promise of victory.

Franklin D. Roosevelt

The Four Freedoms

Beyond the war lies the peace. Both sides have sketched the outlines of the new world toward which they strain. The leaders of the Axis countries have published their design for all to read. They promise a world in which the conquered peoples will live out their lives in the service of their masters.

The United Nations, now engaged in a common cause, have also published their design, and have committed certain common aims to writing. They plan a world in which men stand straight and walk free, free not of all human trouble but free of the fear of despotic power, free to develop as individuals, free to conduct and shape their affairs. Such a world has been more dream than reality, more hope than fact; but it has been the best hope men have had and the one for which they have most consistently shown themselves willing to die.

This free-ness, this liberty, this precious thing men love and mean to save, is the good granite ledge on which the United Nations now propose to raise their new world after victory. The purpose of this pamphlet is to examine and define the essential freedoms.

To talk of war aims, shouting over the din of battle while the planet rocks and vibrates, may seem futile to some. Yet the talk must go on among free peoples. The faith people have in themselves is what the free have to build upon. Such faith is basic to them — man's hot belief in man, a belief which suggests that human beings are capable of ordering their affairs. This is a high compliment paid by man to himself, an evidence or gesture of self-respect, of stature, of dignity, and of worth, an affidavit of individual responsibility.

The freedoms we are fighting for, we who are free: the freedoms for which the men and women in the concentration camps and prisons and in the dark streets of the subjugated countries wait, are four in number.

"The first is freedom of speech and expression — everywhere in the world.

"The second is freedom of every person to worship God in his own way — everywhere in the world.

"The third is freedom from want — which, translated into world terms, means economic understandings which will secure to every nation a healthy peacetime life for its inhabitants — everywhere in the world.

"The fourth is freedom from fear — which, translated into world terms, means a world-wide reduction of armaments to such a point and in such a thorough fashion that no nation will be in a position to commit an act of physical aggression against any neighbor   anywhere in the world."[1]

These freedoms are separate, but not independent. Each one relies upon all the others. Each supports the whole, which is liberty. When one is missing all the others are jeopardized. A person who lives under a tyrant, and has lost freedom of speech, must necessarily be tortured by fear. A person who is in great want is usually also in great fear — fear of even direr want and greater insecurity. A person denied the right to worship in his own way has thereby lost the knack of free speech, for unless he is free to exercise his religious conscience, his privilege of free speech (even though not specifically denied) is meaningless. A person tortured with fears has lost both the privilege of free speech and the strength to supply himself with his needs. Clearly these four freedoms are as closely related, as dependent one upon another, as the four seasons of the natural year, whose winter snows irrigate the spring, and whose dead leaves, fermenting, rebuild the soil for summer's yield.

The first two freedoms — freedom of speech and freedom of religion — are cultural. They are prerogatives of the thinking man, of the creative and civilized human being. Sometimes, as in the United States, they are guaranteed by organic law. They are rather clearly understood, and the laws protecting them are continually being revised and adjusted to preserve their basic meaning. Freedom from fear and from want, on the other hand, are not part of our culture but part of our environment — they concern the facts of our lives rather than the thoughts of our minds. Men are unafraid, or well-fed, or both, according to the conditions under which they live.

To be free a man must live in a society which has relieved those curious pressures which conspire to make men slaves: pressure of a despotic government, pressure of intolerance, pressure of want. The declaration of the four freedoms, therefore, is not a promise of a gift which, under certain conditions, the people will receive; it is a declaration of a design which the people themselves may execute.

1 Franklin D. Roosevelt to the Seventy-seventh Congress, January 6, 1941.

Freedom, of whatever sort, is relative. Nations united by a common effort to create a better world are obviously not projecting a Utopia in which nobody shall want for anything. That is not the point — nor within the range of human possibility. What unites them is the purpose to create a world in which no one need want for the minimum necessities of an orderly and decent life, for cleanliness, for self-respect and security. It is an ambitious design, perhaps too ambitious for the cynic or the faithless; but it is supported by the sure knowledge that the earth produces abundantly and that men are already in possession of the tools which could realize such a purpose if men chose to use them.

This, then, is a credo to which the representatives of 28 nations have subscribed — not a promise made by any group of men to any other group. It is only the people themselves who can create the conditions favoring these essential freedoms which they are now repurchasing in the bazaar of war and paying for with their lives. Nothing is for sale at bargain prices, nor will the house be built in three days with cheap labor. From a world in ruins there can rise only a slow, deliberate monument. This time, conceived by so many peoples of united purpose, it will rise straight upward and rest on good support.

Freedom of Speech

To live free a man must speak openly: gag him and he becomes either servile or full or cankers. Free government is then the most realistic kind of government for it not only assumes that a man has something on his mind, but concedes his right to say it. It permits him to talk — not without fear of contradiction, but without fear of punishment.

There can be no people's rule unless there is talk. Men, it turns out, breathe through their minds well as through their lungs, and there must be a circulation of ideas as well as of air. Since nothing is likely to be more distasteful to a man than the opinion of someone who disagrees with him, it does the race credit that it has so stubbornly defended the principle of free speech. But if a man knows anything at all, he knows that principle is fundamental in self government, the whole purpose of which is to reflect and affirm the will of the people.

In America, free speech and a free press were the first things the minds of the people turned to after the fashioning of the Constitution. Farsighted men, in those early days, readily understood that some sort of protection was necessary. Thus when the first amendment to the Constitution was drawn (part of what the world now knows as the Bill of Rights), it prohibited the Congress from making any law which might abridge the freedom of speech or of the press, or the right of the people peaceably to assemble and to petition the government for a redress of their grievances.

In the Nazi state, freedom of speech and expression have been discarded — not for temporary military expediency, but as a principle of life. Being contemptuous of the individual, and secretly suspicious of him, the German leader has deprived him of his voice. Ideas are what tyrants most fear. To set up a despotic state, the first step is to get rid of the talkers — the talkers in schools, the talkers in forums, the talkers in political rallies and in trade union meetings, the talkers on the radio and in the newsreels, and in the barber shops and village garages. Talk does not fit the Nazi and Fascist scheme, where all ideas are, by the very nature of the political structure, the property of one man.

Talk is death to tyranny, for it can easily clarify a political position which the ruler may prefer to becloud, and it can expose injustices which he may choose to obscure.

Our Bill of Rights specifically mentioned the press. Today the press is one of many forms of utterance. Talk and ideas flow in ever-increasing torrents, through books, magazines, schools, the radio, the motion picture. The camera has created a whole new language of its own.

All these new forms are safeguarded with the ancient guarantees, but the essential danger of not being allowed to speak freely remains. Today the privilege is challenged more gravely than ever before; in the countries dominated by the Axis books are burned, universities are shut down, men are put to death for listening to a radio broadcast. Hitler's New Order seeks to prove that unity and efficiency are achieved most readily among people who are prevented from reading, thinking, talking, debating. This new anesthesia is a subtle drug. Under its quick influence men sleep a strange sleep.

The right to speak, the right to hear, the right of access to information carry with them certain responsibilities. Certain favorable conditions are necessary before freedom of speech acquires validity.

The first condition is that the individual have something to say. Literacy is a prerequisite of free speech, and gives it point. Denied education, denied information, suppressed or enslaved, people grow sluggish; their opinions are hardly worth the high privilege of release. Similarly, those who live in terror or in destitution, even though no specific control is placed upon their speech, are as good as gagged.

Another condition necessary for free speech is that the people have access to the means of uttering it — to newspapers, to the radio, the public forum. When power or capital are concentrated, when the press is too closely the property of narrow interests, then freedom suffers. There is no freedom, either, unless facts are within reach, unless information is made available. And a final condition of free speech is that there be no penalties attached to the spread of information and to the expression of opinion, whether those penalties be applied by the Government or by any private interests whatsoever.

The operation of a free press and the free expression of opinion are far from absolute rights. The laws of libel and slander set limits on what men may say of other men. The exigency of war sets limits on what information may be given out, lest it give aid and comfort to the enemy. Good taste sets limits on all speech.

Freedom of speech, Justice Holmes has warned, does not grant the right to shout fire in a crowded theatre. When ideas become overt acts against peace and order, then the Government presumes to interfere with free speech. The burden of proof, however, is upon those who would restrict speech — the danger must be not some vague danger but real and immediate.

We are not so much concerned with these inevitable limitations to free speech as with the delight at the principle in society and how greatly it has strengthened man's spirit, how steadily it has enlarged his culture and his world. We in America know what the privilege is because we have lived with it for a century and a half. Talk founded the Union, nurtured it, and preserved it. The dissenter, the disbeliever, the crack-pot, the reformer, those who would pull down as well as build up — all are free to have their say.

Talk is our daily fare — the white-bosomed lecturer regaling the Tuesday Ladies' Club, the prisoner at the bar testifying in his own behalf, the editorial writer complaining of civic abuses, the actor declaiming behind the footlights, the movie star speaking on the screen, the librarian dispensing the accumulated talk of ages, the professor holding forth to his students, the debating society, the meeting of the aldermen, the minister in the pulpit, the traveler in the smoking car, the soap-box orator with his flag and his bundle of epigrams, the opinions of the solemn magistrate and the opinions of the animated mouse — words, ideas, in a never-ending stream, from the enduring wisdom of the great and the good to the puniest thought troubling the feeblest brain. All are listened to, all add up to something and we call it the rule of the people, the people who are free to say the words.

The United States fights to preserve this heritage, which is the very essence of the Four Freedoms. How, unless there is freedom of speech, can freedom of religion or freedom from want or freedom from fear be realized? The enemies of all liberty flourish and grow strong in the dark of enforced silence.

For the right to be articulate the inarticulate airman climbs to his fabulous battleground. For this fight the grim-lipped soldier; the close-mouthed sailor; the marine.

Freedom of Religion

That part of man which is called the spirit and which belongs only to himself and to his God, is of the very first concern in designing a free world. It was not their stomachs but their immortal souls which brought the first settlers to America's shores, and they prayed before they ate. Freedom of conscience, the right to worship God, is part of our soil and of the sky above this continent.

Freedom of worship implies that the individual has a source of moral values which transcends the immediate necessities of the community, however important these may be. It is one thing to pay taxes to the state — this men will do; it is another to submit their consciences to the state — this they politely decline. The wise community respects this mysterious quality in the individual, and makes its plans accordingly.

The democratic guarantee of freedom of worship is not in the nature of a grant — it is in the nature of an admission. It is the state admitting that the spirit soars in illimitable regions beyond the collectors of customs. It was Tom Paine, one of the great voices of freedom in early America, who pointed out that a government could no more grant to man the liberty to worship God than it could grant to God the liberty of receiving such worship.

The miracle which democracy has achieved is that while practicing many kinds of worship, we nevertheless achieve social unity and peace. And so we have the impressive spectacle, which is with us always here in America, of men attending many different churches, but the same town meeting, the same political forum.

Opposed to this democratic conception of man and of the human spirit is the totalitarian conception. The Axis powers pretend that they own all of a man, including his conscience. It was inevitable that the Nazis should try to deny the Christian church, because in virtually every respect its teachings are in opposition to the Nazi ideal of race supremacy and of the subordination of the individual. Christianity could only be an annoyance and a threat to Hitler's bid for power and his contempt for the common man.

Today the struggle of Man's spirit is against new and curious shackles. Today a new monstrosity has shown itself on earth, a seven days' wonder, a new child of tyranny — a political religion in which the leader of the state becomes, himself, an object of worship and reverence and in which the individual becomes a corpuscle in the blood of the community, almost without identity. This Nazi freak must fail, if only because men are not clods, because the spirit does live. In the design for a new and better world, religious freedom is a fundamental prop.

We of the nations united in war, among whom all the great religions are represented, see a triumphant peace by which all races will continue the belief in man, the belief in his elusive and untouchable spirit, and in the solid worth of human life.

Freedom from Want

The proposal that want be abolished from this world would be pretentious, or even ridiculous, were it not for two important recent discoveries.

One is the discovery that, beyond any doubt, men now possess the technical ability to produce in great abundance the necessities of daily life — enough for everyone. This is a revolutionary and quite unprecedented condition on earth, which stimulates the imagination and quickens the blood.

Another is the discovery (or rather the realization) that the earth is one planet indivisible — that one man's hunger is every other man's hunger. We know now that the world must be looked at whole if men are to enjoy the fruits they are now able to produce, and if the inhabitants of the globe are to survive and prosper.

Freedom from want, everywhere in the world, is within the grasp of men. It has never been quite within their grasp before. Prosperous times have been enjoyed in certain regions of the world at certain periods in history, but local prosperity was usually achieved at the expense of some other region, which was being impoverished, and the spectre of impending war hung over all. Now, the industrial changes of the last 150 years and the new prospect implicit in the words "United Nations" have given meaning to the phrase "freedom from want" and rendered it not only possible but necessary.

It was in the year 1492 that the earth became round in the minds of men — although it had been privately globular for many centuries. Now in the year 1942, by a coincidence which should fortify astrologers, the earth's rotundity again opens new vistas, this time not of fabulous continents ready to be ransacked, but of a fabulous world ready to be unified and restored. War having achieved totality, against men's wishes but with their full participation, our great resolve as we go to battle must now be that the peace shall be total also. The world is all one today. No military gesture anywhere on earth, however trivial, has been without consequence everywhere; and what is true of the military is true, also, of the economic. A hungry man in Cambodia is a threat to the well-fed of Duluth.

People are worried about the period which will follow this war. Some fear the peace more than they fear the war. But the picture is neither hopeless nor is it black. Already, in this country and abroad, agencies are at work making preliminary studies and designing machinery to stabilize the peacetime world which will follow the war. They are preparing to reemploy the returning soldier, to maintain buying power at a high level, to stand behind industry while it is changing back to peaceable products, to guarantee a certain security to the groups which need such guarantees. The fact that these plans are being drawn is itself encouraging, for when trouble is anticipated and fairly faced, it is less likely to ensue.

The tools of production and the skills which men possess are tremendous in the present war emergency, and when the peace comes, the world will contain more skilled people than ever before in history. Those who are at work planning broadly for a better human society propose to equip this enormous productive manpower with new ideas to fit new conditions.

The pattern is already beginning to become apparent. Once, the soil was regarded as something to use and get the most from and then abandon. Now it is something to conserve and replenish. Once it was enough that a man compete freely in business, for the greatest possible personal gain; now his enterprise, still free, must meet social standards and must not tend toward concentration of power unfavorable to the general well-being of the community. Once, an idle man was presumed to be a loafer; now it is realized he may be a victim of circumstances in which all share, and for which all are responsible.

The great civilizations of the past were never free from widespread poverty. Very few of them, and these only during short periods, produced enough wealth to make possible a decent living standard for all their members, even if that wealth had been equally divided. In the short space of a few decades we have changed scarcity to abundance and are now engaged in the experiment of trying to live with our new and as yet unmanageable riches. The problem becomes one not of production but of distribution and of consumption; and since buying power must be earned, freedom from want becomes freedom from mass unemployment, plus freedom from penury for those individuals unable to work.

In our United States the Federal Government, being the common meeting ground of all interests and the final agency of the people, assumes a certain responsibility for the solution of economic problems. This is not a new role for the Government, which has been engaged since the earliest days of our history in devising laws and machinery and techniques for promoting the well-being of the citizen, whether he was a soldier returning from a war, or a new settler heading west to seek his fortune, or a manufacturer looking for a market for his goods, or a farmer puzzled over a problem in animal husbandry.

The beginning has been made. The right to work. The right to fair pay. The right to adequate food, clothing, shelter, medical care. The right to security. The right to live in an atmosphere of free enterprise. We state these things as "rights" — not because man has any natural right to be nourished and sheltered, not because the world owes any man a living, but because unless man succeeds in filling these primary needs his only development is backward and downward, his only growth malignant, and his last resource war.

All of these opportunities are not in the American record yet, and they are not yet in the world's portfolio in the shape of blueprints. Much of America and most of the world are not properly fed, clothed, housed. But there has never been a time, since the world began, when the hope of providing the essentials of life to every living man and woman and child has been so good, or when the necessity has been so great.

It can be done. The wealth exists in the earth, the power exists in the hills, men have the tools and the training. What remains to be seen is whether they have the wit and the moral character to work together and to lay aside their personal greed.

We and our allies are fighting today not merely to defend an honorable past and old slogans and faiths, but to construct a still more honorable and rewarding future. Fighting men, coming back from the war, will not be satisfied with a mere guarantee of dull security — they will expect to find useful work and a vigorous life. Already moves are being made to meet this inescapable challenge.

The first step, obviously, will be to prevent the sort of slump which has usually followed a great war. War is tremendously costly, in terms of money. Billions are being spent in order that we may win. The peace, too, will be costly, and nothing is gained by evading the fact. But a democracy which can organize itself to defeat one sort of enemy is capable of sustaining the effort through the days that follow. Work, in vast quantity and in infinite variety, will be waiting to be done. We will have the capacity to produce the highest national income ever known, and the jobs to keep men at work.

Freedom from want is neither a conjurer's trick nor a madman's dream. The earth has never known it, nor anything approaching it. But free men do not accept the defeatist notion that it never will. The freeing of all people from want is a continuing experiment, the oldest and most absorbing one in the laboratory, the one that has produced the strangest gases and the loudest explosions. It is a people's own experiment and goes on through the courtesy of chemists and physicists and poets and technicians and men of strong faith and unshakable resolve.

Freedom from Fear

Fear is the inheritance of every animal, and man is no exception. Our children fear the tangible dark, and we give them what reassurance we can, so that they will grow and develop normally, their minds free from imaginary terrors. This reassurance, this sense of protection and security, is an important factor in their lives.

The new dark which has settled on the earth with the coming of might and force and evil has terrified grown men and women. They fear the dark, fear fire and the sword; they are tormented by the dread of evils which are only too real. They fear the conqueror who places his shackles on the mind. Above all else they are tortured by that basic political fear: fear of domination of themselves by others — others who are stronger, others who are advancing, others who have the weapons and are destroying and burning and pillaging. This is the fear which haunts millions of men and women everywhere in the world. It is the fear of being awakened in the night, with the rapping on the door.

No structure of peace, no design for a good world, will have any solidity or strength or even any meaning unless it disperses the shadow of this fear and brings reassurance to men and women, not only for themselves but for their children and their children's children. Aggressive war, sudden armed attack, secret police, these must be forever circumvented. The use of force, historically the means of settling disputes, must be made less and less feasible on earth, until it finally becomes impossible. Even though the underlying causes which foment wars may not be immediately eradicated from the earth, the physical act of war can be prevented when people, by their ingenuity, their intelligence, their memory, and their moral nature, choose to do so. Force can be eliminated as a means of political action only if it be opposed with an equal or greater force — which is economic and moral and which is backed by collective police power, so that in a community of nations no one nation or group of nations will have the opportunity to commit acts of aggression against any neighbor, anywhere in the world.

The machinery for enforcing peace is important and indispensable; but even more important is that there be established a moral situation, which will support and operate this machinery. As the last war ended, an attempt was made to construct an orderly world society capable of self-control. It was an idealistic and revolutionary plan. But like the first automobile, it moved haltingly and was more of a novelty than a success. For a while men's hopes focused on the plan; but it was never universally accepted. The faith was not there, nor the courage.

Today many nations are working together with unbelievable energy and with harmony of feeling and interest. They are united at the moment by the desire to win battles, but they are also united by common principles and by a conviction that their people ultimately want the same thing from life — freedom, peace, security, the chance to live as individuals.

Such collaboration has its origin in the democratic spirit, which infects men regardless of latitude or longitude, and it has been fed by the close association between nations which are geographically near neighbors — as, for example, the inter-American powers. Canada has been a good neighbor to the United States for many years, and the Canadian border, never fortified, stands today as a symbol of what the world will be when men's faith becomes great enough and their heads become hard enough.

Still another answer to fear is found in the concept of the United Nations. For the first time in history, twenty-eight nations have been acting together, in the very midst of a mortal struggle, to set down the specifications of a peace settlement and the aims of war and post-war action. Their representatives, meeting in Washington on New Year's Day, 1942, signed a historic Declaration by United Nations, saying:

"The Governments signatory hereto,

"Having subscribed to a common program of purposes and principles embodied in the Joint Declaration of the President of the United States of America and the Prime Minister of the United Kingdom of Great Britain and Northern Ireland dated August 14, 1941, known as the Atlantic Charter,

"Being convinced that complete victory over their enemies is essential to defend life, liberty, independence and religious freedom, and to preserve human rights and justice in their own lands as well as in other lands, and that they are now engaged in a common struggle against savage and brutal forces seeking to subjugate the world,

Declare:

"(1) Each Government pledges itself to employ its full resources, military or economic, against those members of the Tripartite Pact and its adherents with which such government is at war.

"(2) Each Government pledges itself to cooperate with the Governments signatory hereto and not to make a separate armistice or peace with the enemies.

"The foregoing declaration may be adhered to by other nations which are, or which may be, rendering material assistance and contributions in the struggle for victory over Hitlerism."

The nations signing the Declaration by United Nations are: The United Kingdom of Great Britain and Northern Ireland, the Union of Soviet Socialist Republics, China, Australia, Belgium, Canada, Costa Rica, Cuba, Czechoslovakia, the Dominican Republic, El Salvador, Greece, Guatemala, Haiti, Honduras, India, Luxembourg, the Netherlands, New Zealand, Nicaragua, Norway,

Panama, Poland, South Africa, Yugoslavia, and the United States of America. On June 14, Mexico and the Philippine Islands adhered to the Declaration by United Nations.

Can anyone be deaf to the sound of hope in this assemblage? Men have not achieved their goal, but at least they have collectively aspired to it, and have accepted a responsibility for it which is continuing and not merely fitful. The work is to go on. The new building will indeed be built, whatever its shape, whatever its appointments, whatever its defects.

Those are the goals of the peace and the hope of the world. But the specific and immediate problem, the first move to free people from fear, is to achieve a peaceable world which has been deprived of its power to destroy itself. This can only be accomplished by disarming the aggressors and keeping them disarmed. Last time they were disarmed, but they were not prevented from rearming. This time they will be disarmed in truth.

It will be remembered that the inquisitive Ben Franklin, testing the lightning with his kite, found in the storm's noisy violence the glimmerings of a secret which later illuminated the world. His example suggests that good news is sometimes hidden in bad weather. Today, in the storm which rages across the whole earth, men are sending up their kites to the new lightning, to try its possibilities and to prepare for clearing skies.

The Four Freedoms guide them on. Freedom of speech and religion, freedom from want and from fear — these belong to all the earth and to all men everywhere. Our own country, with its ideas of equality, is an experiment which has been conducted against odds and with much patience and, best of all, with some success for most people. It has prospered and brought fresh hope to millions and new good to humanity. Even in the thick of war the experiment goes ahead with old values and new forms. Life is change. The earth shrinks in upon itself and we adjust to a world in motion, holding fast to the truth as we know it, confident that as long as the love of freedom shows in the eyes of men, it will show also in their deeds.

Freedom of Speech
Booth Tarkington

In a small chalet on the mountain road from Verona to Innsbruck, two furtive tourists sat, pretending not to study each other. Outdoors, the great hills rose in peace that summer evening in 1912; indoors, the two remaining patrons, both young, both dusty from the road, sat across the room from each other, each supping at his own small table.

One was of robustly active figure, dark, with a bull head; the other was thin and mouse-haired. It was somewhat surprising to see him take from his knapsack several sketches in water color. Upon this, the dark young traveler, who'd been scribbling notes in a memorandum book, decided to speak.

"You're a painter, I see."

"Yes," the insignificant one replied, his small eyes singularly hard and cold. "You, sir, I take to be a writer?"

The dark young man brought his glass of red wine and his plate of cheese and hard sausage to the painter's table. "You permit?" he asked as he sat down. "By profession I am a journalist."

"An editor, I think," the water color painter responded. "I might guess that you've written editorials not relished by the authorities."

"Why do you guess that?"

"Because," the painter said, "when other guests were here, a shabby man slipped in and whispered to you. A small thing, but I observed it, though I am not a detective."

"Not a detective," the dark young man repeated. "And yet perhaps dangerously observant. This suggests that possibly you do a little in a conspiratorial way yourself."

"Why do you say that?"

"Because of your appearance. You're precisely a person nobody would notice, but you have an uneasy yet coldly purposeful eye. And because behind us it's only a step over the mountain path to Switzerland, where political refugees are safe."

"Yes, no doubt fortunately for you!" The mouse-haired painter smiled. "As for me I am in no trouble with the authorities, but I admit that I have certain ideas."

"I was sure you have." The journalist drank half his wine. "Ideas? With such men as you and me that means ambitions. Socialism, of course. That would be a first step only toward what we really want. Am I right?"

"Here in this lonely place" — the painter smiled faintly —"it is safe to admit that one has dazzling thoughts. You and I, strangers and met by chance, perceive that each in his own country seeks an extreme amount of success. That means power. That is what we really want. We are two queer men. Should we both perhaps be rightly thought insane?"

"Greatness is easily mistaken for insanity," the swarthy young man said. "Greatness is the ability to reduce the most intricate facts to simple terms. For instance, take fighting. Success is obtained by putting your enemy off his guard, then striking him where he is weakest — in the back, if possible. War is as simple as that."

"Yes, and so is politics," the painter assented absently as he ate some of the fruit that formed his supper. "Our mutual under-standing of greatness helps to show that we are not lunatics, but only a simple matter of geography is needed to prove our sanity."

"Geography?" The journalist didn't follow this thought. "How so?"

"Imagine a map." The painter ate a grape. "Put yourself in England, for instance, and put me and my dazzling ideas into that polyglot zoo, the United States of America. You in England can bel-low attacks on the government till you wear out your larynx, and some people will agree with you and some won't, and that is all that would happen. In America I could do the same. Do you not agree?"

"Certainly," the journalist said. "In those countries the people create their own governments. They make them what they please, and so the people really are the governments. They let anybody stand up and say what he thinks. If they believe he's said some-thing sensible, they vote to do what he suggests. If they think he is foolish they vote no. Those countries are poor fields for such as you and me, because why conspire in a wine cellar to change laws that permit themselves to be changed openly?"

"Exactly." The water-color painter smiled his faint strange smile. "Speech is the expression of thought and will. Therefore, freedom of speech means freedom of the people. If you prevent them from expressing their will in speech, you have them enchained, an absolute monarchy. Of course, nowadays he who chains the people is called a dictator."

"My friend!" the dark young man exclaimed. "We understand each other. But where men cannot speak out, they will whisper. You and I will have to talk out of the sides of our mouths until we have established the revolutions we contemplate. For a moment, suppose us successful. We are dictators, let us say. Then in our turn do we permit no freedom of speech? If we don't, men will talk out of the sides of their mouths against us. So they may overthrow us in turn. You see the problem?"

"Yes, my friend. Like everything else, it is simple. In America or England, so long as governments actually exist by means of freedom of speech, you and I could not even get started; and when we shall have become masters of our own countries, we shall not be able to last a day unless we destroy freedom of speech. The answer is this: we do destroy it."

"But how?"

"By means of purge."

"Purge?" The word seemed new to the journalist. "What is that?"

Once more was seen the water-color painter's peculiarly icy smile. "My friend, if I had a brother who talked against me, either out of the side of his mouth or the front of it, and lived to run away, he might have to leave his wife and child behind him. A purge is a form of carbolic acid that would include the wife and child."

"I see." The dark youth looked admiring, but shivered slightly. "On the one hand, then, there is freedom of speech and on the other this fatal acid you call a purge. The two cannot exist together in the same country. The people of the earth can take their choice, but you and I can succeed only where we persuade them to choose the purge. They would be brainless to make such a choice — utterly brainless!"

"On the other hand," said the painter, "many people can be talked into anything, even if it is terrible for themselves. I shall flatter all the millions of my own people into accepting me and the purge instead of freedom."

He spoke with a confidence so monstrous in one of his commonplace and ungifted appearance that the other stared aghast. At this moment, however, a shrill whistle was heard outside. Without another word the dark young man rose, woke the landlord, paid his score and departed hurriedly.

The painter spoke to the landlord: "That fellow seems to be some sort of shady character, rather a weak one. Do you know him?"

"Yes and no," the landlord replied. "He's in and out, mainly after dark. One meets all sorts of people in the Brenner Pass. You might run across him here again, yourself, someday. I don't know his whole name, but I have heard him called 'Benito,' my dear young Herr Hitler."

Freedom of Worship
Will Durant

Down in the valley below the hill where I spend my summers is a little white church whose steeple has been my guiding goal in many a pleasant walk.

Often, as I passed the door on weekdays when all was silent there, I wished that I might enter, sit quietly in one of the empty pews, and feel more deeply the wonder and the longing that had built such chapels — temples and mosques and great cathedrals — everywhere on the earth.

Man differs from the animal in two things: he laughs, and he prays. Perhaps the animal laughs when he plays, and prays when he begs or mourns; we shall never know any soul but our own, and never that. But the mark of man is that he beats his head against the riddle of life, knows his infinite weakness of body and mind, lifts up his heart to a hidden presence and power, and finds in his faith a beacon of heartening hope, a pillar of strength for his fragile decency.

These men of the fields, coming from afar in the uncomfortable finery of a Sabbath morn, greeting one another with bluff cordiality, entering to worship their God in their own fashion — I think, sometimes, that they know more than I shall ever find in all my books. They have no words to tell me what they know, but that is because religion, like music, lives in a world beyond words, or thoughts, or things. They have felt the mystery of consciousness within themselves, and will not say that they are machines. They have seen the growth of the soil and the child, they have stood in awe amid the swelling fields, in the humming and teeming woods, and they have sensed in every cell and atom the same creative power that wells up in their own striving and fulfillment. Their unmoved faces conceal a silent thankfulness for the rich increase of summer, the mortal loveliness of autumn and the gay resurrection of the spring. They have watched patiently the movement of the stars, and found in them a majestic order so harmoniously regular that our ears would hear its music were it not eternal. Their tired eyes have known the ineffable splendor of earth and sky, even in tempest, terror and destruction; and they have never doubted that in this beauty some sense and meaning dwell. They have seen death, and reached beyond it with their hope.

And so they worship. The poetry of their ritual redeems the prose of their daily toil; the prayers they pray are secret summonses to their better selves; the songs they sing are shouts of joy in their refreshened strength. The commandments they receive, through which they can live with one another in order and peace, come to them as the imperatives of an inescapable deity, not as the edicts of questionable men. Through these commands they are made part of a divine drama, and their harassed lives take on a scope and dignity that cannot be canceled out by death.

This little church is the first and final symbol of America. For men came across the sea not merely to find new soil for their plows but to win freedom for their souls, to think and speak and worship as they would. This is the freedom men value most of all; for this they have borne countless persecutions and fought more bravely than for food or gold. These men coming out of their chapel — what is the finest thing about them, next to their undiscourageable life? It is that they do not demand that others should worship as they do, or even that others should worship at all. In that waving valley are some who have not come to this service. It is not held against them; mutely these worshipers understand that faith takes many forms, and that men name with diverse words the hope that in their hearts is one.

It is astonishing and inspiring that after all the bloodshed of history this land should house in fellowship a hundred religions and a hundred doubts. This is with us an already ancient heritage; and because we knew such freedom of worship from our birth, we took it for granted and expected it of all mature men. Until yesterday the whole civilized world seemed secure in that liberty.

But now suddenly, through some paranoiac mania of racial superiority, or some obscene sadism of political strategy, persecution is renewed, and men are commanded to render unto Caesar the things that are Caesar's, and unto Caesar the things that are God's. The Japanese, who once made all things beautiful, begin to exclude from their realm every faith but the childish belief in the divinity of their emperor. The Italians, who twice littered their peninsula with genius, are compelled to oppress a handful of hunted men. The French, once honored in every land for civilization and courtesy, hand over desolate refugees to the coldest murderers that history has ever known. The Germans, who once made the world their debtors in science, scholarship, philosophy and music, are prodded into one of the bitterest persecutions in all the annals of savagery by men who seem to delight in human misery, who openly pledge themselves to destroy Christianity, who seem resolved to leave their people no religion but war, and no God but the state.

It is incredible that such reactionary madness can express the mind and heart of an adult nation. A man's dealings with his God should be a sacred thing, inviolable by any potentate. No ruler has yet existed who was wise enough to instruct a saint; and a good man who is not great is a hundred times more precious than a great man who is not good. Therefore, when we denounce the imprisonment of the heroic Niemöller, the silencing of the brave Faulhaber, we are defending the freedom of the German people as well as of the human spirit everywhere. When we yield our sons to war, it is in the trust that their sacrifice will bring to us and our allies no inch of alien soil, no selfish monopoly of the world's resources or trade, but only the privilege of winning for all peoples the most precious gifts in the orbit of life — freedom of body and soul, of movement and enterprise, of thought and utterance, of faith and worship, of hope and charity, of a humane fellowship with all men.

If our sons and brothers accomplish this, if by their toil and suffering they can carry to all mankind the boon and stimulus of an ordered liberty, it will be an achievement beside which all the triumphs of Alexander, Caesar and Napoleon will be a little thing. To that purpose they are offering their youth and their blood. To that purpose and to them we others, regretting that we cannot stand beside them, dedicate the remainder of our lives.

Freedom from Want
Carlos Bulosan

If you want to know what we are, look upon the farms or upon the hard pavements of the city. You usually see us working or waiting for work, and your think you know us, but our outward guise is more deceptive than our history.

Our history has many strands of fear and hope, that snarl and converge at several points in time and space. We clear the forest and the mountains of the land. We cross the river and the wind. We harness wild beast and living steel. We celebrate labor, wisdom, peace of the soul.

When our crops are burned or plowed under, we are angry and confused. Sometimes we ask if this is the real America. Sometimes we watch our long shadows and doubt the future. But we have learned to emulate our ideals from these trials. We know there were men who came and stayed to build America. We know they came because there is something in America that they needed, and which needed them.

We march on, though sometimes strange moods fill our children. Our march toward security and peace is the march of freedom — the freedom that we should like to become a living part of. It is the dignity of the individual to live in a society of free men, where the spirit of understanding and belief exist; of understanding that all men are equal; that all men, whatever their color, race, religion or estate, should be given equal opportunity to serve themselves and each other according to their needs and abilities.

But we are not really free unless we use what we produce. So long as the fruit of our labor is denied us, so long will want manifest itself in a world of slaves. It is only when we have plenty to eat — plenty of everything — that we begin to understand what freedom means. To us, freedom is not an intangible thing. When we have enough to eat, then we are healthy enough to enjoy what we eat. Then we have the time and ability to read and think and discuss things. Then we are not merely living but also becoming a creative part of life. It is only then that we become a growing part of democracy.

We do not take democracy for granted. We feel it grow in our working together — many millions of us working toward a common purpose. If it took us several decades of sacrifices to arrive at this faith, it is because it took us that long to know what part of America is ours.

Our faith has been shaken many times, and now it is put to question. Our faith is a living thing, and it can be crippled or chained. It can be killed by denying us enough food or clothing, by blasting away our personalities and keeping us in constant fear. Unless we are properly prepared, the powers of darkness will have good reason to catch us unaware and trample our lives.

The totalitarian nations hate democracy. They hate us, because we ask for a definite guaranty of freedom of religion, freedom of expression and freedom from fear and want. Our challenge to tyranny is the depth of our faith in a democracy worth defending. Although they spread lies about us, the way of life we cherish is not dead. The American dream is only hidden away, and it will push its way up and grow again.

We have moved down the years steadily toward the practice of democracy. We become animate in the growth of Kansas wheat or in the ring of Mississippi rain. We tremble in the strong winds of the Great Lakes. We cut timbers in Oregon just as the wild flowers blossom in Maine. We are multitudes in Pennsylvania mines, in Alaskan canneries. We are millions from Puget Sound to Florida. In violent factories, crowded tenements, teeming cities. Our numbers increase as the war revolves into years and increases hunger, disease, death and fear.

But sometimes we wonder if we are really a part of America. We recognize the mainsprings of American democracy in our right to form unions and bargain through them collectively, our opportunity to sell our products at reasonable prices, and the privilege of our children to attend schools where they learn the truth about the world in which they live. We also recognize the forces which have been trying to falsify American history — the forces which drive many Americans to a corner of compromise with those who would distort the ideals of men that died for freedom.

Sometimes we walk across the land looking for something to hold on to. We cannot believe that the resources of this country are exhausted. Even when we see our children suffer humiliations, we cannot believe that America has no more place for us. We realize that what is wrong is not in our system of government, but in the ideals which were blasted away by a materialistic age. We know that we can truly find and identify ourselves with a living tradition if we walk proudly in familiar streets. It is a great honor to walk on the American earth.

If you want to know what we are, look at the men reading books, searching in the dark pages of history for the lost word, the key to the mystery of living peace. We are factory hands, field hands, mill hands, searching, building and molding structures. We are doctors, scientists, chemists, discovering and eliminating disease, hunger and antagonism. We are soldiers, Navy men, citizens, guarding the imperishable dream of our fathers to live in freedom. We are the living dream of dead men. We are the living spirit of free men.

Everywhere we are on the march, passing through darkness into a sphere of economic peace. When we have the freedom to think and discuss things without fear, when peace and security are assured, when the futures of our children are ensured — then we have resurrected and cultivated the early beginnings of democracy. And America lives and becomes a growing part of our aspirations again.

We have been marching for the last one hundred and fifty years. We sacrifice our individual liberties, and sometimes we fail and suffer. Sometimes we divide into separate groups and our methods conflict, though we all aim at one common goal. The significant thing is that we march on without turning back. What we want is peace, not violence. We know that we thrive and prosper only in peace.

We are bleeding where clubs are smashing heads, where bayonets are gleaming. We are fighting where the bullet is crashing upon armorless citizens, where the tear gas is choking unprotected children. Under the lynch trees, amidst hysterical mobs. Where the prisoner is beaten to confess a crime he did not commit. Where the honest man is hanged because he told the truth.

We are the sufferers who suffer for natural love of man for another man, who commemorate the humanities of every man. We are the creators of abundance.

We are the desires of anonymous men. We are the subways of suffering, the well of dignities. We are the living testament of a flowering race.

But our march to freedom is not complete unless want is annihilated. The America we hope to see is not merely a physical but also a spiritual and an intellectual world. We are the mirror of what America is. If America wants us to be living and free, then we must be living and free. If we fail, then America fails.

What do we want? We want complete security and peace. We want to share the promises and fruits of American life. We want to be free from fear and hunger.

If you want to know what we are — We are Marching!

Freedom from Fear
Stephen Vincent Benét

What do we mean when we say "freedom from fear"? It isn't just a formula or a set of words. It's a look in the eyes and a feeling in the heart and a thing to be won against odds. It goes to the roots of life — to a man and a woman and their children and the home they can make and keep.

Fear has walked at man's heels through many ages — fear of wild beasts and wilder nature, fear of the inexplicable gods of thunder and lightning, fear of his neighbor man.

He saw his rooftree burned with fire from heaven — and did not know why. He saw his children die of plague — and did not know why. He saw them starve, he saw them made slaves. It happened — he did not know why. Those things had always happened.

Then he set himself to find out — first one thing, then another. Slowly, through centuries, he fought his battle with fear. And wise men and teachers arose to help him in the battle.

His children and he did not have to die of plague. His children and he did not have to make human sacrifices to appease the wrath of inexplicable gods. His children and he did not have to kill the stranger just because he was a stranger. His children and he did not have to be slaves. And the shape of Fear grew less.

No one man did this by himself. It took many men and women, over many years. It took saints and martyrs and prophets — and the common people. It started with the first fire in the first cave — the fire that scared away the beasts of the night. It will not end with the conquest of far planets.

Since our nation began, men and women have come here for just that freedom — freedom from the fear that lies at the heart of every unjust law, of every tyrannical exercise of power by one man over another man. They came from every stock — the men who had seen the face of tyranny, the men who wanted room to breathe and a chance to be men. And the cranks and the starry-eyed came, too, to build Zion and New Harmony and Americanopolis and the states and cities that perished before they lived — the valuable cranks who push the world ahead an inch. And a lot of it never happened, but we did make a free nation.

"How are you ever going to live out there, stranger?"

"We'll live on weevily wheat and the free air." If they had the free air, they'd put up with the weevily wheat.

So, in our corner of the world, and for most of our people, we got rid of certain fears. We got rid of them, we got used to being rid of them. It took struggle and fighting and a lot of working things out. But a hundred and thirty million people lived at peace with one another and ran their own government. And because they were free from fear, they were able to live better, by and large and on the whole, than any hundred and thirty million people had lived before. Because fear may drive a burdened man for a mile, but it is only freedom that makes his load light for the long carry.

And meanwhile around us the world grew smaller and smaller. If you looked at it on the school maps, yes, it looked like the same big world with a big, safe corner for us. But all the time invention and mechanical skill were making it smaller and smaller. When the Wright brothers made their first flights at Kittyhawk, the world shrank. With those first flights the world began to come together and distant nations to jostle their neighbor nations.

Now, again in our time, we know Fear — armed Fear, droning through the sky. It's a different sound from the war whoop and the shot in the lonesome clearing, and yet it is much the same for all of us. It is quiet in the house tonight and the children are asleep. But innocence, good will, distance, peaceable intent, will not keep those children safe from the fear in the sky. No one man can keep his house safe in a shrunken world. No one man can make his own clearing and say "This is mine. Keep out." And yet, if the world is to go on, if man is to survive and prosper, the house of man must be kept safe.

So, what do we mean by "freedom from fear"?

We do not mean freedom from responsibility — freedom from struggle and toil, from hardship and danger. We do not intend to breed a race wrapped in cotton wool, too delicate to stand rough weather. In any world of man that we can imagine, fear and the conquest of fear must play a part.

But we have the chance, if we have the brains and the courage, to destroy the worst fears that harry man today — the fear of starving to death, the fear of being a slave, the fear of being stamped into the dust because he is one kind of man and not another, the fear of unprovoked attack and ghastly death for himself and for his children because of the greed and power of willful and evil men and deluded nations.

It will not be easy to destroy those fears. No one man can do it alone. No one nation can do it alone. It must be all men.

It is not enough to say, "Here, in our country, we are strong. Let the rest of the world sink or swim. We can take care of ourselves." That may have been true at one time, but it is no longer true. We are not an island in space, but a continent in the world. While the air is the air, the bomb can kill your children and mine. Fear and ignorance a thousand miles away may spread pestilence in our own town. A war between nations on the other side of the globe may endanger all we love and cherish.

War, famine, disease are no longer local problems or even national problems. They are problems that concern the whole world and every man. That is a hard lesson to learn, and yet, for our own survival, we must learn it.

A hundred and sixty odd years ago, we, as a nation, asserted that all men were created equal, that all men were entitled to life, liberty and the pursuit of happiness. Those were large assertions, but we have tried to live up to them. We have not always succeeded, we have often failed. But our will and desire as a nation have been to live up to them.

Now, in concert with other free nations, we say that those children you see and other children like them all over the world shall grow to manhood and womanhood free from fear. We say that neither their minds nor their bodies shall be cramped or distorted or broken by tyranny and oppression. We say they shall have a chance, and an equal chance, to grow and develop and lead the lives they choose to lead, not lives mapped out for them by a master. And we say that freedom for ourselves involves freedom for others — that it is a universal right, neither lightly given by providence nor to be maintained by words alone, but by acts and deeds and living.

We who are alive today did not make our free institutions. We got them from the men of the past and we hold them in trust for the future. Should we put ease and selfishness above them, that trust will fail and we shall lose all, not a portion or a degree of liberty, but all that has been built for us and all that we hope to build. Real peace will not be won with one victory. It can be won only by long determination, firm resolve and a wish to share and work with other men, no matter what their race or creed or condition. And yet, we do have the choice. We can have freedom from fear.

Here is a house, a woman, a man, their children. They are not free from life and the obligations of life. But they can be free from fear. All over the world, they can be free from fear. And we know they are not yet free.

Grateful acknowledgment is made for permission to reproduce the following images and excerpts in this book, and for assistance with their use. All Norman Rockwell art work appears courtesy of © 1993 The Norman Rockwell Family Trust. All photographs courtesy of the Norman Rockwell Museum at Stockbridge, unless otherwise noted.

1 *Roosevelt and Seventy-Seventh Congress*. Courtesy of the Franklin D. Roosevelt Library. Reproduced courtesy of Wide World Photos, Inc. **4** *Draft of Four Freedoms speech*. Courtesy of the Franklin D. Roosevelt Library. **8** *Roosevelt and Churchill*. Courtesy of the Franklin D. Roosevelt Library. **9** *Atlantic Charter*. Courtesy of the Franklin D. Roosevelt Library. **10** *Arlington town meeting report*. From the Arlington, Vermont, Town Clerk. **15** *Rockwell and Let's Give Him Enough*. Courtesy of NYT Pictures. Photograph by Gene Pelham. **21** *Washington, D.C.* Courtesy of the Franklin D. Roosevelt Library. **25-26** *Excerpt from* Norman Rockwell: My Adventures as an Illustrator. New York: Harry N. Abrams, 1988. By Norman Rockwell, with Thomas Rockwell. **30** *Rockwell and Speech*. (Also on the back cover). National Archives; from Summary Report of Four Freedoms War Bond Show. **38** *OWI Four Freedoms pamphlet cover*. National Archives. **40** *The Freedoms Conquer, William Soles*. Fine Prints Collection, Library of Congress. **41** *The Four Freedoms, Ralph Fabri*. Fine Prints Collection, Library of Congress. **42** *Four Freedoms photomontage, Jean Carlu*. Courtesy of the Franklin D. Roosevelt Library. **43** *Four Freedoms mural, Hugo Ballin*. Courtesy of the City of Burbank, California. Photograph by Floyd Faxon Commercial Photography. **Color section** *Freedom of Speech, Freedom of Worship, Freedom from Want, Freedom from Fear* (also on the front cover).

Photography by Paul Rocheleau. *Freedom of Worship preliminary idea ("Barbershop").* © 1990 Sotheby's, Inc. *Study for Freedom of Speech ("Town Meeting").* Courtesy of the Metropolitan Museum of Art, George A. Hearn Fund, 1952. *Photo of the Rockwell Family.* © 1943 Curtis Publishing Co. *Poster versions of Mine America's Coal and Hasten The Homecoming.* Courtesy of the Franklin D. Roosevelt Library. **55** *Aunt Jennie's Store.* National Archives. **59** *Quote from* The Crosswinds of Freedom *by James MacGregor Burns.* New York: Alfred A. Knopf, 1989. **63ff** *Letters.* From the Norman Rockwell Archive, collection of the Norman Rockwell Museum at Stockbridge. **73** *Post advertisement in Chicago Tribune.* © 1943 Curtis Publishing Co. **75** *This is Nazi Brutality, Ben Shahn.* Courtesy of the Franklin D. Roosevelt Library. **76** *Hecht's advertisement in Washington Post.* Courtesy of Hecht's, a division of the May Department Stores Company. **80** *Commemorative cover.* National Archives. **81** *Saturday Evening Post store window display.* National Archives. **85** *Strawbridge and Clothier exhibition salon.* Courtesy of Strawbridge and Clothier. **85** *Will Durant and Worship.* National Archives; from Summary Report. **86** *Models in radio broadcast and publicity photo.* Courtesy Shirley McTernan/Arlington Gallery. **87** *Hengerer Company scenes.* National Archives; from Summary Report. **89** *Carson Pirie Scott advertisement* in *Chicago Tribune.* Courtesy of Carson Pirie Scott, a division of P.A. Burgner & Co. **90** *Holmes store scene.* National Archives; from Summary Report. **91** *Bullock's advertisement in Los Angeles Times.* Courtesy of R.H. Macy & Co., Inc. **98** *Norman Rockwell Museum, Stockbridge.* Peter Aaron/Esto. **125ff** *Text of Post essays.* © 1943 Curtis Publishing Co..

Bibliography

Norman Rockwell and the Four Freedoms

Alexander, Jack. "Cover Man." *The Saturday Evening Post* (February 13, 1943).

Buechner, Thomas. *Norman Rockwell, Artist and Illustrator*. New York: Harry N. Abrams, 1970.

Cohn, Jan. *Creating America: George Horace Lorimer and the Saturday Evening Post*. Pittsburgh: University of Pittsburgh Press, 1989.

"The Four Freedoms." *The Saturday Evening Post* (February 20, 27, March 6, 13, 1943).

Guptill, Arthur L. *Norman Rockwell Illustrator*. New York: Watson-Guptill Publications, 1946.

Jarman, Rufus. "Profiles U.S. Artist." *The New Yorker* (March 17, 24, 1945).

Meyer, Susan E. *Norman Rockwell's People*. New York: Harry M. Abrams, 1981.

Meyer, Susan E. *Norman Rockwell's World War II: Impressions from the Homefront*. USAA Foundation, 1991.

Olsen, Lester C. "Portraits in Praise of a People: A Rhetorical Analysis of Norman Rockwell's Icons in Franklin D. Roosevelt's Four Freedoms Campaign." *Quarterly Journal of Speech* 69 (1983), 15-24.

Ratcliffe, Carter. "Barnet Newman: Citizen of the Infinitely Small Republic." *Art in America* 79:92-7 (Spring 1991).

Rockwell, Norman, with Thomas Rockwell. *Norman Rockwell: My Adventures as an Illustrator*. New York: Harry N. Abrams, 1988.

Franklin D. Roosevelt's Four Freedoms and World War II History

Braden, Waldo W., and Brandenburg, Ernest. "Roosevelt's Fireside Chats." *Speech Monographs* 22:5 (November, 1955).

Burns, James MacGregor. *The Crosswinds of Freedom*. New York: Alfred A. Knopf, 1989.

Burns, James MacGregor. *Roosevelt: The Lion and the Fox*. New York: Harcourt Brace World, 1956.

Burns, James MacGregor. *Roosevelt: The Soldier of Freedom*. New York: Harcourt Brace Jovanovich, Inc., 1970.

Crowell, Laura. "The Building of the Four Freedoms Speech." *Speech Monographs* 22:5 (November, 1955).

Moynihan, Daniel P. "The 50th Anniversary of President Franklin Delano Roosevelt's Four Freedoms Speech." Address delivered in Lyndon B. Johnson Room, United States Capitol, Washington, D.C., January 30, 1991. Printed text of speech from FDR Library, Hyde Park, NY.

Rosenman, Samuel I. *Working with Roosevelt*. New York: Harper & Brothers, 1952.

Sherwood, Robert E. *Roosevelt and Hopkins: An Intimate History*. New York: Harper & Brothers, 1948.

War Art

Art Trade Journals including *American Artist, Art Digest, Design*.

Art and Psychological Warfare: World War II Posters. Hempstead, New York: The Emily Lowe Gallery, February 6 - March 21, 1982 exhibition catalog.

Landau, Ellen. *Artists for Victory*. Washington, D.C.: Library of Congress, February 2 - July 31, 1983 exhibition catalog.

Rhodes, Anthony, and Margolin, Victor, eds. *Propaganda: The Art of Persuasion: World War II.* New York: Chelsea House, 1976, 1983.

Zeman, Zbynek A.B. *Selling the War: Art and Propaganda in World War II.* London: Orbis Books, 1978.

Homefront

Benet, William Rose. "Oh boy, but there's an ocean/ Of joy in promotion" (poem). *Saturday Review* 26 (May 8, 1943).

Blum, John Morton. *Roosevelt and Morganthau.* Boston: Houghton Mifflin, 1970.

Blum, John Morton. *V was for Victory: Politics and American Culture during World War II.* New York: Harcourt Brace Jovanovich, 1976.

Cartwright, Dorwin. "Some Principles of Mass Persuasion: Selected Findings of Research on the Sale of United States War Bonds." *Human Relations,* 1949, 2, 253-267; reprinted in *Public Opinion and Propaganda: A Book of Readings.* New York: The Dryden Press.

Casdorph, Paul D. *Let The Good Times Roll: Life at Home in America During World War Two.* New York: Paragon House, 1989.

Cowley, Malcolm. "The Sorrows of Elmer Davis." Saturday Review (May 3, 1943).

Culbert, David. "Education Unit in World War II: An Interview with Eric Barnouw." *Journal of Popular Culture* 12:2 (Fall 1979).

MacDonald, J. Fred. "Government Propaganda in Commercial Radio — the Case of 'Treasury Star Parade, 1942-3.'" *Journal of Popular Culture* 12:2 (Fall 1979).

Polenberg, Richard. *War and Society: The United States, 1941-1945.* New York: J.B. Lippincott Co., 1972.

"Truth & Trouble." *Time* (March 15, 1943).

Weinberg, Sydney Stahl. "Wartime Propaganda in a Democracy: American Twentieth Century Information Agencies." Columbia University PhD. dissertation, 1969.

Winkler, Allan M. *The Politics of Propaganda: The Office of War Information, 1942-1945.* New Haven: Yale University Press, 1978.

Manuscript and Archival Collections

Norman Rockwell Museum at Stockbridge, Massachusetts
    Norman Rockwell Archive
    Oral Histories, collected by Susan Meyer, James McCabe

The Curtis Archives, Indianapolis, Indiana

Franklin D. Roosevelt Library, Hyde Park, New York
    Stephen G. Early Papers
    Henry Morganthau Jr. Papers
    Peter Odegard Papers
    Franklin D. Roosevelt Papers

Library of Congress, Washington, D.C.
    Elmer Davis Papers
    Archibald MacLeish Papers

National Archives
    Department of the Treasury, War Finance Division
    Office of War Information and predecessor agencies

The Norman Rockwell Museum at Stockbridge exhibits the largest significant public collections of artwork by Norman Rockwell. The museum's principal purpose is to collect, preserve, study, interpret, and present to the public material pertaining to the life and career of Norman Rockwell. The museum is committed to interpreting the broader themes of Rockwell's contributions to illustration and to American popular culture and society.

The museum is the only one founded with the assistance of Norman Rockwell and personally endorsed by the artist, his family, and estate. In 1973, Rockwell left his collection of art in trust to the museum to ensure the collection's future public exhibition and care. Three years later, he added his studio and its contents to the trust. That same year, 1976, the museum began a ten-year research project that resulted in the 1986 publication of *Norman Rockwell: The Definitive Catalogue*, which contains more than 3,500 known images by Rockwell.

The museum moved into a new state-of-the-art museum building, located on a former estate in Stockbridge, in 1993. Norman Rockwell's studio and its contents, in keeping with his wish that his working environment be shared with the public, was moved to the site from Rockwell's home in the town center in 1986 and is now open to museum visitors seasonally.